NOT
~~THAT~~
LIKEABLE

AMANDA HAMILTON

NOT THAT LIKEABLE

a Memoir

AND OTHER STORIES
I TOLD MYSELF

PAGE TWO

Cataloguing in publication information is available from Library and Archives Canada.
ISBN 978-1-77458-014-1 (paperback)
ISBN 978-1-77458-115-5 (ebook)

Page Two
pagetwo.com

Edited by Amanda Lewis and Melissa Edwards
Copyedited by Steph VanderMeulen
Proofread by Alison Strobel
Cover, interior design, and illustrations by Taysia Louie
All photographs courtesy of Amanda Hamilton, except
the photo on page 10, courtesy the *Edmonton Sun*

notthatlikeable.com

To my bullies:
Thank you for your dedicated torment throughout
my formative years. Without you, I might
have been more likeable and deprived of stories
to tell myself, or anyone else for that matter.

With gratitude,
A.

Also, to my family:
Thanks for putting up with all of my shit over
the years. The words I wish I could use to thank
you simply wouldn't do my gratitude justice.
Instead, I made this book, chronicling our shared
weirdness. I really hope I don't get disowned.

With love,
Mandi

"Yes, this is my cool new book. I really have no idea what to write so I guess I could blab on and on forever about nothing. Yeah well, this book is extremely cool if I do say so myself. There is so much to write about, yet I have no idea what to write about first. See, I told you I could babble on and on about nothing. That's a special talent of mine. Feel proud, feel really proud."

AMANDA, Grade 9 diary entry

CONTENTS

Amanda Whalen

INTRODUCTION

I'VE BEEN BABBLING, as I do, about writing a book for quite some time. I recall the exact moment I released this bit of information out into the world, having no idea what I had done to myself. Propped atop a fire-engine-red bar stool at a restaurant I had just finished designing, I made a casual declaration to my client's bar manager, like he would give two shits.

Me, circa forever ago, with not a single word written: "I'm writing a book."

This was not the response he had expected to his "what's up?" question. Dude wasn't looking for a soliloquy—he wanted me to respond with, "Not much. You?"

Bar manager, genuinely caught off guard: "Oh... wow. A book, hey? That's crazy! Uh... do you have a writing background or something?"

In 2017, I was ramping up my business in the Vancouver market (I'd been killing it in Calgary since '07) and had tacked on a solo writing retreat on one of my coastal voyages. I was at an event in the downtown neighbourhood of Gastown, in a furniture store that carries some of the most luxurious brands on the market. The event was on a Thursday evening, and I was due to catch a forty-minute ferry from West Van to a quaint seaside Airbnb the following afternoon. As I opened the freshly Windexed doors of the store and stepped out into the street, there was a palpable contrast. This area, while hip, is also sadly home to a massive drug crisis, and as night falls, the streets become animated with all of the lost souls who congregate, like broken marionettes.

When I returned to my vehicle, I saw that the passenger-side window had been smashed. My work bag with my laptop was gone, and the manuscript (which I had finally made progress on) was not backed up. As someone who was considered moderately tech-savvy and got over 90 percent in her Grade 10 computer class, I appreciate that my behaviour was idiotic and reckless. I was supposed to be leaving in the morning to spend the next four days in an intensive, self-directed writing retreat and I had no laptop and no manuscript. Despite the fact that as a child I had journaled every day with a pencil (gasp!) and paper (whoa!), it never occurred to my adult self to pick up a notebook, which could have made for a very "beta" version of my retreat. *Why* had I not embraced *the cloud*? FFS.

For the next hour, I drove up and down Hastings Street, cutting through menacing back lanes with names like "Blood Alley" (and the more colloquial "Piss Alley") in hopes of finding the hunk of metal that stored my manuscript. To no one's surprise, my laptop never resurfaced. In all likelihood, it had already swapped hands a few times, with the promise of a next hit. RIP, First Draft of *Not That Likeable*.

Money was tight at that time, and the expense of my business endeavour was draining my bank account. After returning to my hotel, which was at best a glorified dorm room, I crawled into an undersized tub with about eight inches of lukewarm bathwater and allowed myself to indulge in self-pity. I sobbed, my tears contaminating the cheap wine I was drinking out of a clear plastic cup. Despite my best efforts to drown my frustrations (and maybe myself) in less than a foot of water, this wretched attempt at feeling sorry for myself ended short of ten minutes. As I stared at my distorted body in the chrome reflection of the bathtub faucet, I didn't like what I saw. Whether it's vanity or self-preservation, I've never been very liberal with my tears, and pride snapped me out of my stupor. Nothing was going to stop me. Early the next morning, with luggage and a new laptop in hand, I was off to Gibsons to write.

Best known for the long-running CBC television show *The Beachcombers*, Gibsons is a sleepy town located on the Sunshine Coast of British Columbia. As my editor and I so eloquently put it, it's the type of place where "palo santo smoke curls from the double chimney of log homes and hippies' tears drip from burnished brass taps with a patina that matches the moss accumulating on the side of the roof." We aren't being indulgent, it's simply the truth.

The writing retreat was situated on a lush property that stretched in all directions and was home to several horses, donkeys, llamas, chickens, dogs, cats, and, most impressively, a muster of peafowl. My room was atop the owner's free-standing art studio and gallery and included a large garage door that opened to the yard, allowing the salty ocean air to waft into the creative space I would call home for the next few days. Each morning, I was roused by the shrill call of the peacocks as they flirted, displaying their striking plumage and fanning their colourful tails. A basket of fresh muffins from the local bakery and a hot chai latte would adorn my doorstep, along with a light layer of dew. With renewed optimism and freshly purchased Post-its, I started the outline of my book—again.

About six weeks later, my laptop was stolen from my vehicle again (how many times do I have to write "again"?). I know what you're thinking... *Why does this chick keep leaving her laptop in her car with a big red sign that says, "STEAL ME"?* But guess what? This time it was all backed up—on "the cloud"—and instead of crying in a bathtub, I was laughing in disbelief. The universe had an awfully fucked up way of testing me once I had finally committed to writing my book. On the plus side, the thief had the decency to return the remaining contents of my work bag, which held all of my corporate balance sheets, my passport, and my Nexus card, to the steps of a nearby legal office. Had this thief been shrewder, they might have stolen my identity instead of my shitty first draft.

For the next year or so, I casually kicked at my manuscript—until, in late 2019, I finally got serious about it. Not long after, about a month into the pandemic lockdown, I had the grossly mistaken idea that I'd have more time to write and so I committed to my publisher, Page Two. This was not the case. With a booming housing market, more people working from home and refocusing their energy on renovations, and well-funded commercial projects continuing to push forward, my business was growing exponentially. In addition to a very demanding work schedule, I had a geriatric dog who was going through expensive health procedures, requiring a lot of extra care. Then, weeks away from turning in my manuscript for the first round of editing, the world I knew shifted well beyond anything I could have ever expected from the pandemic.

Returning home late from an impromptu visit with friends, my husband and I were both a touch tipsy from the perfectly chilled Meursault we had been sharing while sitting around the fireplace. I had just hauled the cool white sheets over my warm limbs when he dropped a bomb.

"Babe?"

You know, *that* type of "Babe"—the one that ends in a precariously placed question mark so you just fucking know that whatever follows is *really* going to suck. My heart sank into an oak barrel. A million thoughts boot-stomped the wine grapes that were now going straight to my head. This brain pigeage included: *Has he finally lost it with all of the vintage glassware I keep buying? I mean, you need different types of glassware depending on the drink. A good host knows this.* Or maybe: *I bet one of my dried-up contacts that I haphazardly flicked on the floor before bed is lodged into his foot. He hates it when that happens. I'm kinda a slob. I should stop doing that.*

He didn't wait for me to answer.

"I need to talk to you about something important."

Does he want to have sex? When did I last shower? I really wish he'd given me some warning so I could have snagged that stray hair from my left nip.

I sat up in the dark, quickly assessing that it was *very* much like my husband to broach something grim in the silence of the night. Perhaps the darkness acted as a calm harbour for his spirited emotions, pushing up like waves against a sturdy hull in the night. He announced that he wanted to separate.

As I reflect on the tears I shed throughout the process of our separation, I realize that, ultimately, I never could have imagined how the pain of ending this relationship would be so aligned with the pain of exploring my youth in such a deeply intimate way. This book would not have been possible without the access I had to my childhood diaries, each of which unearthed long-buried memories and truths that, in large part, had evolved in my mind along the way. The stories in this book, as well as the ones I have long told myself, explore a continual questioning of my self-worth. I have always been looking to find a sense of place and fulfil a deep need to feel accepted. And I can see now that my relentless pursuit to be likeable and to avoid rejection drove me to unknowingly indulge in self-sabotaging behaviour in so many ways. I was a bit weird, rather outspoken, and frequently the catalyst for horrifying, self-inflicted teenage drama. Dazzled by the potential of being liked, I put on displays of antics— and, in doing so, innocently invited bullies into my world. Perhaps this feels familiar. In my naivety, I was determined to obtain the approval of others. The process of pushing all these stories from memory and my old diary pages into this book— all through a divorce, managing a growing business, falling in love and then out of love again, and occasionally losing my manuscript—has taught me more than my editor would want me to share on these pages. Perhaps that's a second book.

And now, in a classic Amanda move, I'm going to change the subject and deflect with a bit of humour. If you bought this book to support me and have no intention of reading it, well, thanks, friend. You may want to consider skimming the first chapter, "The Chronology of Becoming Likeable," or, if you feel so inclined to read on, pick one later in the book. That way, next time we meet, you can impress me by saying things like, "Bangs... am I right?!" or inquire more about Number 31: "Have the two of you stayed in contact?"

Are you ready for poop jokes yet? I am. I hope that you see a little bit of yourself in these stories and laugh a lot along the way. At me, for me, with me, in spite of me. Let's do this.

xx,
Amanda

P.S. SHOULD ANYTHING in this book offend you or if you were among those who fell victim to any of my childish tirades, I invite you to email me for a formal apology at sorry@notthatlikeable.com.

1

THE CHRONOLOGY OF BECOMING LIKEABLE

"Allright Deb! I bought some wine and I'll be drinking it for you tonight. Love always, D + C"

NOTE IN BABY SHOWER CARD, Amanda's baby book
(Mom's friends knew how to party.)

"It's about time! Congrats Debby! Sandi"

NOTE IN BABY SHOWER CARD, Amanda's baby book
(Apparently Mom has been trying to be a teen mom for a while now.)

1981: Conceived during the Klondike Days, which are held each year in Edmonton, Alberta. Luckily, this act was *not* with a carnie. My mom swears it actually happened in Coeur d'Alene, Idaho, on a perch where locals would cliff dive. I'm told that my biological father had come down on his motorcycle, and, according to Mom, she had "not been doing the pill thing properly and pretty much got pregnant on the *first-ish* time." With my grandparents following behind in their car, my mom returned home to Edmonton on the back of my dad's motorcycle in the pissing rain, wearing a green garbage bag to protect herself from the elements. I mean, it all sounds pretty romantic, if you ask me. I also think it's a reasonable fact to point out on my application should I ever want to pursue American citizenship.

1982: I enter the world early at 10:21 and on 4/20, of all days. The former is laughable because I spend the rest of my life in a persistent state of lateness. The latter makes me a real disappointment to the "four-twenty" community given that, at the time of writing this book, I still have never participated in the enjoyment of "The Marijuana." I did, however, attend a house party in Grade 12 where the entire property was hotboxed *and* I do have a pot cookie in my freezer (with a layer of frostbite and the word "medicinal" scribbled across the front of the Ziploc bag in Sharpie). This birthdate makes me an Aries–Taurus cusp (google that shit, it's *terrifying*). I also share my birthday with Hitler, the Columbine High School Massacre of '99, and, during COVID, the crash of crude oil prices falling into the red for the first time in history. That's a lot of awfulness in one day.

1983: August 7, on his Serious Moonlight Tour, David Bowie performs for over sixty thousand people at the Commonwealth Stadium in Edmonton. Like a bobblehead on a car dashboard, I sit atop my mom's shoulders while she and her boyfriend, Mike, rock out to "Space Oddity," "Let's Dance," and "Young Americans." Mom gets busted going in with a Coleman cooler that she had filled with pink lemonade. Apparently, she had used a sack of quarters to weigh down the bottle of vodka she was hiding at the bottom of the cooler. Ingenious.

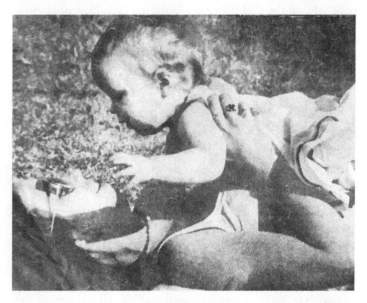

1983. First birthday, Mom and me in the park.

1984: I turn my grandparents' living room into an art project by painting their white walls with my mom's nail polish.

1985: After her term at the Est-elle Academy of Hair Design, my mom introduces me to bangs, which results in a lifetime addiction to this face-framing fringe and the still-held notion that my forehead is much too large. I wake up early the next day and escape from the window of our basement apartment to go for a solo joyride on my tricycle down a busy street to show off my new bangs. Mom isn't impressed.

1986: I fall down the steep staircase leading to the rumpus room of my grandparents' home. I was mimicking my uncle Bobby's usual rapid descent down the sharp, narrow flight, rotating a little to the left to ensure greater foot-to-tread coverage. The tactic was entirely unnecessary—I had child-sized feet (I still do today). My impersonation of Uncle Bobby was a literal and figurative attempt at trying to find my footing at a young age. I end up rupturing my appendix and need emergency surgery. According to my baby book, I "recuperate quickly to the playroom in the hospital." Like many children, I blame my family for this incident, or, more specifically, my uncle Bobby, for his zestful approach to descending the stairs at warp speed. (Growing up in a household of *Star Trek* fans and being subjected to endless hours of James T. Kirk will undoubtedly result in numerous space-related metaphors throughout this book. I do not expect you to respect them in the slightest. Live long and prosper. 🖖)

1987: My devotion to apple juice begins.

1988: I befriend a girl named Andrea who lives across the alley. We become immediate besties and attend Grade 1 at St. Gabriel Elementary School together. I spend most of the year with my name in Mrs. C's "ChatterBox" on the blackboard.

Despite my public shaming, my school diary reflects over and over that I loved Mrs. C, I loved myself, I loved Andrea, I loved my mom, and I loved my dad (even though my dad was not in the picture).

1989: I switch schools to attend Holy Family Catholic Elementary School, where my grandmother works and is able to keep me under close watch. It's the only time in my life that I'm popular, and it is solely because all of the younger kids think it's very cool that my grandma is the principal. She wakes me at 6 a.m. every day so that we can eat breakfast together at a restaurant before school starts. Later, during summer break—sailing with the world's finest skipper, my grandfather—my family gifts me the nickname "Stinky Feet" after I forget to bring socks with me. Apparently, salty toes barefoot in a pair of Velcro kicks for ten days results in a very unsavoury stench.

1990: I "borrow" ketchup chips and vanilla ice cream cups (you know, the ones with the wooden spoons) from the kitchen after school. My early dabbles with soft-core theft end here. *SimCity* makes its way into my hands via the sons of my Grade 3 teacher, Mrs. P. I spend a lot of time building underpowered cities with minimal infrastructure to make more room for parks and malls, taxing the shit out of the citizens, and then ultimately triggering a natural disaster when I grow tired of my creation. I suspect that the residents of my city did not find me all that likeable.

1991: Switching to Julia Kiniski School, I start Grade 4 with my aunt Karen as my teacher. She and her teacher friends make fun of my outfits, giggling over the garish combinations of colour and pattern that I boldly present to the student body each day.

TOP **1989. Aunt Karen and me; the birth of "Stinky Feet."**

BOTTOM **1991. The Canadian Tuxedo. Very cool.**

1992. *Looney Tunes* and stuffies. Lammy on the left.

1992: A big fan of *The Lion, the Witch and the Wardrobe* by C.S. Lewis, I'm delighted to try my first Turkish Delight. But unlike Edmund in the story, I don't fall for the White Witch's tawdry games. I have a collection of stuffed lambs, my favourite being Lammy. Lammy comes to school with me each day, dressed in threads hand-sewn by none other than *moi* and "holding" his own collection of textbooks. I separate my desk from all the other students and teach Lammy alongside my Grade 5 teacher's lesson plans. Quebec threatens to separate from the rest of Canada, and I become unreasonably worried about this isolating my grandparents' hometown in the Maritimes. I learn how to handwrite, which, like my temporary popularity, starts to wane swiftly in relevance. Also, the contents of my diaries take a swift turn. I'm officially boy crazy.

1993: My grandmother, who had previously accepted a promotion working "downtown" at the Edmonton Catholic School District, demotes herself and returns to work as a principal at St. Teresa Catholic Elementary School. She's my ride, so I join her for Grade 6. I quickly learn that at this age, it is 100 percent no longer cool to be the granddaughter of the principal. I would have had more luck being the preacher's daughter, and it certainly would have garnered a few more dates with the bad boys.

1994: My parents opt to send me to a performing arts school then called Victoria Composite Junior High. There are silverfish in my gym locker, which is located in the school's grimy basement, and I'm convinced the whole place is haunted. I believe that Moist is a dirty word the kids are saying, unaware it's a very popular grunge band. Save for one friend, who is as dorky as I am, I am immensely unpopular.

1995: Bye, Vic Comp! Hello, St. Kevin Catholic Junior High! This does not help my cool factor. In some alternate universe, I might have been cool had I acquired a rap sheet that explained my transient educational experience, gaining me some street cred with the popular kids. Instead, my records merely show standardized test scores that illustrate consistently poor math skills. I fall for a girl who shares my name and has unbearably high pants (apparently—as she likes to say— due in part to a short torso), and we become lifelong friends.

1996: My first kiss. His name is Benny, and he is the class clown. We smooch atop a stained mattress, which has been stripped of its sheets and wedged into the corner of a room against the cool concrete walls of the basement foundation of his divorced mother's house. Despite the creepy interior, I'm crushing hard on him and imagine myself surrounded by fresh rose petals and lit candles overwhelming the room in profuse vanilla scents. He touches my left boob. Prudish, inexperienced, and ill prepared, I'm mortified and leave abruptly.

1997: I start high school at Austin O'Brien Catholic with many of my classmates from junior high. I'm dating a boy, Jim, who is two years older than me and attends another school. Hoping my classmates will see him, I feel *very* cool when Jim picks me up from school in his *own car*. To save face, I don't mention that we are both dorks who sing in a choir together.

1998: I steal my grandmother's champagne-coloured Nissan 240SX and take it for a joyride. I incorrectly exit from a traffic circle but respond in kind to the anger of the other drivers by honking, cursing, and giving them the finger. I get caught by my uncle David, who must have seen me jerking around the neighbourhood as I rode the clutch and awkwardly transitioned between first and second gear. I need to stop hanging out with the older kids.

1999: I get elected student council president—not because I'm popular but because my entire campaign rides on the fact that my competitor, Corey, plays on the football team, and "he just simply won't have time to take this seriously, you know, with all of that practice and those away games." Meanwhile, I'm so overinvested in extracurricular activities that I almost flunk out of high school.

1995. Amanda and Amanda, both very into bangs.

2000: Benny (the boob toucher) and I are on round two and are now going steady. The weekend before I turn eighteen, we party at his dad's place in Beaumont, which is on the outskirts of Edmonton and is just as creepy as his mom's basement. The house is, at best, a glorified shed—a tiny structure located on a large undeveloped lot. We blast rap music and I drink two Mike's Hard Lemonade coolers. Benny drives me home and I scream the lyrics to Eiffel 65's "Blue (Da Ba Dee)" out of his dad's F150 truck, which doubles as our semi-private make-out room. When I return home, I crank the squeaky front door open and am met by my grandmother's floral muumuu. She is either oblivious or chooses to completely disregard my mild intoxication.

2

THE WHELAN CLAN

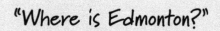

"Where is Edmonton?"

EVERYONE IN THE WORLD, circa 1985

GROWING UP in Edmonton, the capital of Alberta, typically means being repeatedly buried under a blanket of snow, making for desolate, miserable winters. The only respite from six-plus months of five-foot-tall snow piles surrounding your lot was the promise of a visit to the city's claim to fame: the indoor water park at the West Edmonton Mall. The largest in the world at the time and boasting an average 31 degrees Celsius, this tropical oasis features seventeen slides, many of which caused me great emotional distress for fear that, on the way down, I might shit myself (a fear that grew into a lifelong concern) or lose a boob from my one-piece swimsuit. All in, the mall comprises 5.3 million square feet and contains more than eight hundred retail stores and services, including two hotels, more than a hundred dining venues, an indoor skating rink, a zipline, and a marine centre. When I was a preteen, my grandmother and aunt would let me stay overnight at the hotel for my birthday and I would select a different themed room each year, my favourite being the Hollywood room. (I seem to recall the glam interiors having little lights embedded in the carpet. Today, the room boasts a stripper pole.) But my favourite attraction by far was Galaxyland. Previously called Fantasyland (until 1995 as a result of a Disney lawsuit), the indoor playground has over twenty-seven rides, including four roller coasters. Much to my grandmother's disapproval, my mother introduced me to the best one: the Mindbender. My grandmother's concerns were fully justified—three people died after one of the cars derailed in 1986.

While "The Mall" takes all the credit for being the number one tourist attraction in Edmonton, the city's real charm can be found in the 160 kilometres of pathways that weave throughout the river valley, and in the long-standing and iconic Fringe theatre festival. With its thriving arts community, Edmonton definitely doesn't get the reputation it deserves—at least, one beyond the garish allure of the mall's sad indoor dolphins, theme rooms, and stale cotton candy.

Our home was located in the quietly average community of Fulton Place, wedged like an afterthought between the neighbourhood of Capilano and the Capilano Mall. Unlike "The Mall," Capilano's shopping centre was a depressed building that was, at best, a last kick at the can for the failing businesses that probably got paid to take over the otherwise empty retail space. Small groups of senior citizens would glide across the dirty linoleum floors in scuffed white Reeboks, pacing up and down the large main corridor, getting their doctor-prescribed steps in, safe from the frigid Edmonton weather.

Monolithic apartment towers faced in "gloom"-coloured stucco and dotted with junk-filled balconies circled the neighbouring communities, broken up by surface parking lots, strip malls, and a long-standing local pub called the Rex Tavern. Legend has it that my mother, along with her boyfriend, Leon, and their cronies, smoked darts and drank Budweiser on tap there until the ugly lights came on. Infinitely creative, she claims she earned $300 by giving names to several of the feature shooters at the bar and for designing the poster that advertised them. The Rex would dole out these same shots to my mother on demand, frequently regretting their generosity when she proceeded to perform gymnastics—specifically, back walkovers—on the bar and then consumed the shots like a stuntwoman for the locals.

While it lacked the colour of an indoor amusement park or the culture of a grassroots arts festival, the neighbourhood of Capilano became my playground for "cops and robbers" and endless bike rides and Slurpee runs as my childhood bestie, Andrea, and I terrorized a community that likely wasn't the ideal backdrop for supporting free-range kids. When asked, I would twist the truth and say I lived in the nearby, and more affluent, neighbourhood of Gold Bar, where my friend Kristen lived. The homes there rolled into a ravine that led down to the North Saskatchewan River. We would often get lost in those trees as we hiked through to loiter in the park the way only teenage girls know how to do best.

Yards in Gold Bar were expertly manicured, the green lawns mowed in a flawless checkerboard pattern and bordered by well-maintained white picket fences. Perennial flowers bloomed in a recurrent cycle at the hands of seasoned gardeners—ranunculus and tulips in the spring; hydrangeas and lilacs perfuming the summers. Autumn was always a mystery as we anticipated when the first dump of snow would fall and ruin the freesias and all hell would freeze over in Edmonton.

Hailing from Cape Breton, Nova Scotia, my grandparents purchased our classic beige-coloured bungalow in 1969 for $23,000. While the house had nothing more than egg crates for furniture, their sailboat, the *Godolphin*, named after the renowned horse in the book *King of the Wind*, sat in the backyard. Our house had one washroom and would end up housing seven humans: the Whelan Clan. This elite circle included my grandmother and grandfather, my mother (whom everyone called "the Deb"), my aunt Karen, my uncle David, and my uncle Bobby—second oldest to my mother. Catapulted into being a father figure, it was Uncle Bobby who was in charge of constantly entertaining me as a young child. After I arrived home from school each day, I would find him tinkering with the engine of his treasured Mercury Monarch, and I'd harass him for a box of Smarties until he agreed to take me to the corner store. Each evening he'd bounce me up and down on his bad "Whelan knees" while we indulged in the antics of Admiral Kirk as he travelled back in time to do things like save the earth with the help of an old Klingon Bird-of-Prey.

A key battleground in this crowded house was the washroom, and we would all scrap over who was occupying the toilet for great lengths of time. Sadly, it was my uncle David who got the worst of my banging at the door—he and I seemed to be on the same bathroom schedule. My grandpa would say things like, "How long is it going to take for you to put your face on?" or "Turn off the goddamn lights, will ya." Our home was—*is*—situated on an extra-wide lot that allowed both for a lane between the house and the single-car garage and for oversized yards, front and back. The rear yard, heavily treed, provided adequate privacy for the numerous times when my overactive bladder and excessive apple juice consumption got the best of me and I would need to pop a squat.

With his East Coast roots, baby-blue eyes, and freckles that were strewn like seashells awash on a beach, my grandfather always had a sentence or two on what it was like to live through the Depression. He and my grandmother grew up chewing on tar, so anytime I disagreed with their perspectives, I would remind them that they had consumed a significant quantity of benzene and should have sprung for shares in Dubble Bubble. My grandpa grew up in a very poor family, and my grandmother was adopted into a wealthy

**Our house had
one washroom and
would end up housing
seven humans:
the Whelan Clan.**

family and spent her youth dancing around her pet pony and sleeping alongside her porcelain dolls.

The main floor of our house featured three bedrooms and was designed to allow riotous children (my mother, aunt, and uncles—and, now, me) to run circles around a central partition that separated the kitchen and dining room from the living space. My grandfather built three additional bedrooms in the basement to house the rest of the family. My bedroom, previously the basement entertainment room, was rather large and featured a fake brick fireplace that stretched wall to wall and acted as storage for my growing Barbie collection. Like the cave that it is, it still bears the marks of crayon petroglyphs today.

Despite the support of this extensive multi-generational clan, at no point was it easy for my teen mom when she found she was *with child* at seventeen. Even today, "the Deb" swears that abortion was never an option, that she *chose* me. You and I both know she's full of shit, but I pander to her fabulist version of my conception. While Catholic guilt whispers in the undertow of this familial ship, this is one time I can be thankful for its shameless prowess. Mom, capable of fighting a priest, never forgave the church for apparently wanting to do a "back door" baptism for her bastard child. She and my dad were both young and their relationship did not end on good terms. After an attempt at solo-parenting me for a couple of years, my mom eventually moved in with my grandparents. She was stubborn by nature, and, as she says, "there was no goddamn way" she was going to share custody with her "sperm donor." Let's be clear about this: my mom is cray and she knows it. It's why we love her—she brings vibrant colour into an overwhelmingly muted world of people surrendering to conformity in every last bullshit thing. The Deb is the original *Free Spirit*. Patchouli-toting, crystals-in-your-bralette-wearing hippies, bow down.

Since both my grandparents were working full time to support this family of seven and my mom was busy working split shifts, I was predominantly raised by my mother's siblings, who at the time were only in their late teens and early twenties. When I speak of "my parents," this includes all of these adults—it really did take a village to raise me. I hold the unique dynamic of being an only child with many parents, a pseudo-sibling to my aunt and uncles, an occasional sister and girlfriend to my mother, both a daughter and granddaughter to my grandparents, and, as I found out later in life, a half-sister to my father's two sons.

For all of these various titles, my primary role was that of "royal pain in the ass" to my grandfather. His dreams of retiring at fifty with a healthy combination of crossword puzzles and John Grisham novels was short lived, as he became my primary caregiver, toting me around to soccer games and basketball tournaments and being on pick-up duty when I wanted to hang with my friends, which was basically all the time. It's a long-standing family joke that my grandfather assumes I'm about to ask for something anytime I open my mouth. And when I do make any such request, he can often be found muttering something about "needing a ball-peen hammer." So, like the *obedient* granddaughter that I was, when I redecorated his room for his birthday, I had one installed above the door in his room for easy access.

We are a clan of gifted storytellers, and each member of my family has an inimitable way of shapeshifting events until they are as unrecognizable as the *Star Trek* creatures that rematerialize on the transporter deck of the *Enterprise*. Also, we *really* fucking dig metaphors—especially the sentimental ones that make your stomach turn. Every Christmas Eve, without fail, I would act as the "holiday spirit" skipper, pulling in my familial crew from below deck for a game of Balderdash. It was always met with jeers of disinterest, but, ultimately, I would win everyone over with pity for my over-zealous love of the game. Except we didn't actually *own* Balderdash. We used a dated dictionary, heavy and bound in a cobalt cover that over the years had become so thrashed from being chucked at each other across the living room that it donned a generous strip of duct tape along its spine to keep it appropriately clothed. Eventually, it lost its inhibitions, disrobed, and lost its front cover. To this day, it awkwardly sits naked on a shelf awaiting our next rematch. Like every year before, Balderdash resulted in endless laughter—the men in my family effectuating galactically inspired definitions and the women submitting to metaphorically permissive descriptions, ultimately exposing them all. I was a wild card and often won.

Dinners, generally prepared by my grandfather, still include one of three dishes: Irish stew (my fave), rigatoni with meatballs, and meatloaf. This was remarkably healthier than the sodium-bloated meal my mother typically dished out: Sapporo Ichiban noodles with an egg drop. Often, my grandfather and I would cruise over to the Capilano Mall so that I could enjoy my favourite takeout dish of chicken balls, chop suey, and rice, suffocated by pineapple glaze, all dropped into a Styrofoam to-go container. On special occasions, like the odd Sunday dinner, my grandmother would request a combination of barbecued chicken and salmon, and we would dine alfresco in the backyard, in grass that was high enough to garner complaints from the neighbours. My grandma's culinary talents are expressed exactly three times a year—Easter, Thanksgiving, and Christmas. Attacking a spread that includes 5,812,105 dishes, I would disregard any assumed food placement boundaries and dump everything onto my mashed potatoes, which always occupied, and still do, a minimum of 50 percent of my plate. I am of Irish heritage, after all.

Someone skimped on my mashed potatoes and there is hell to pay.

Our rather unorthodox family structure is akin to that of a wolf pack, trusting each other and protecting each other's survival at all costs. This includes the aforementioned feeding time, particularly holidays. Even today, we still show our true Whelan nature as we hover over the turkey carcass and shovel food into our mouths like barbarians, all the while howling over each other to see who can capture the most attention. Whatever we ate off of during these childhood dinners, whether hand-wash-only pottery or paper plates, both were bordered with floral designs in an attempt to disguise these mealtimes as a civilized family affair. If, on some rare

My primary role was that of "royal pain in the ass."

occasion, you have the opportunity to witness the Whelan Clan in the wild, be prepared for full mouths of food interrupting you without pause, never providing a moment of airspace for you to actually respond. I'm quite certain that what you have to say is very important and very intelligent; it's just that you'll need to learn how to project your voice, lose all manners, and field several questions at once. Multi-tasking is our familial superpower.

In the Whelan household, if you were hungry, you dug through the hall closet for cereal that had not yet expired. If you wanted clean clothes, you threw someone else's wet clothes from the washing machine onto the cool, unfinished concrete floor so you could wash your own. If you needed lunch money, you snuck loonies from grandpa's coin stash while he was sleeping (sorry, Gramps). I'm certain I didn't brush my teeth unless specifically prompted, which might explain the fourteen cavities that were chillin' in my mouth by the time of my first dentist appointment, which didn't take place until I was a teenager. I curbed my own stench by submerging my filthy body in bubbles reeking of lavender and rose blends only ever intended for those of my grandmother's generation.

My school in kindergarten and Grade 1 was just a few blocks from home. My mom walked with me once so that I could learn the route, and from then on, I was on my own. The trek included cutting down a long alley, turning down two more short alleys, and then crossing a major road that had an unmarked crosswalk. I have to hand it to my mom: her approach to parenting was rather fearless (albeit a little naive), and she embedded a sense of self-reliance in me at a very young age. Right from my earliest days at school, I was often responsible for my own laundry and for making sure I had a lunch—except on the occasional days when my mom would make it, in which case there would be a little love note and a fuck-ton of candy in the package. But I never once had to do "real" chores, *ever*. No one had chores in our house, apart from the occasional moments when someone might casually suggest I clean the dishes of rotten food out from underneath my bed to reduce the smell that emanated from my room. My grandparents cared more about my grades than they did the pigsty that was my bedroom. (To be fair, my grotesque display of filth in my youth instilled a manic if inconsistent drive for tidiness in my adult years. Though I am still just a touch of a slob—I stash five-cent candies under my pillow for late-night snacking.)

When I reflect on my memories of growing up, it's my perspective that, for the most part, I had a large hand in raising myself. In many ways, I feel we all did in my family. Perhaps this is a result of my grandparents' laissez-faire parenting style, but it seems that parenting in the Whelan Clan was more like the role of bumpers in a bowling lane, gently preventing me from falling into the gutter along the way. This lack of structure, absence of discipline, and freedom from boundaries resulted in wild independence—which I still practise to a fault. It's a fantastic origin story for an entrepreneur, though it may not have been exactly as I remember it. Even at the worst of times, I feel immeasurably grateful. Hindsight has allowed me to clearly see the guidance, love, and support I have collectively received from the village of people who raised me.

THIS BIRD IS A BITER

"I love the blackness."

AMANDA, age four, writing in the interior of her diary entirely scrawled over in black crayon

THERE WERE OTHER kids like me. You know, the ones who smelled a bit sour and perhaps had parents who didn't love them enough to sacrifice their careers for full-time child-rearing. We were each abandoned at daycare at an age when someone should have been snuggling our stinky, feral little bodies for at least a few more years.

At some point during my time at that daycare, I made a friend. Let's call her Tina, short for Christina, which, like Amanda, was another very popular name for a girl blessed with earthly presence in the '80s. In fact, Christina, along-side Brianne, was another name that my mother considered for me, as she loved the idea of a name that had plenty of room for nicknames. She settled on Amanda (obviously), the full version of which she reserved exclusively for the times when she was appalled by my behaviour—which, with her short temper, was often. She got her nicknames, however: I was, at various times, blessed with "Chucky Chops," "'Pa," "Pumpkin," "Amandichucks," "Squibollus" (sorry, what?), "Mander Panders," "Three-Foot Nothin'," "Punky" (of the television show *Punky Brewster*), "DEMAND-a" (that's a good one), and "Aman-DUH." Usually, she simply referred to me as "Mandi" (my stripper name) and "Pumpkin" (also my stripper name). *Mandi, the pole dancin', pumpkin-lovin' stripper.* (Please make sure to dot the "i" in Mandi with a heart, otherwise you've completely lost the point here. ♡♡♡)

Tina and I became fast friends after she baited me with a promise to share her name-brand fruit snacks. My grandpa, despite his own addiction to Coca-Cola and Oh Henry! chocolate bars, refused to buy "that crap" for me. Every day during recess, Tina and I would play together, attached at the hip, Tina following my bossy lead. The daycare in question reserved its gated front yard for those felonious types of children who were at risk of offending the gen pop of other kids—in other words, kids like me.

On one such day, as I entered this preschool penitentiary, I saw Tina playing with another girl.

Weird. Why wasn't she hanging out with me?

I casually sauntered over to the water table where the two girls were playing.

"Tina, let's go play on the slide," I ventured.

"Um ... no. I'm gonna stay with ... *her.*" *Her,* in this case, was not just this particular girl. *Her* clearly meant any kid other than me.

"Why?"

Glancing at the other girl and avoiding eye contact with me, Tina said, "'Cause you're so bossy."

Bossy! I was stunned. "I'm not bossy," I said back. "*You* never wanna do anything fun!" I rolled my eyes and left Tina with her new friend, tossing my stringy hair, hoping that my long locks would inspire envy and distract Tina from my burning insecurity.

I climbed up on the plastic slide that sat in the yard and perched on top of it, monopolizing the playground's greatest attraction. About three "kid hours" later (read: one minute), I heard a timid voice ask, "You gonna go?"

I whipped my head around to see Tina standing on the steps behind me. I had no idea how long she had been waiting there. Feeling like the kingpin of maximum security, I swung my legs around toward her so that her face was basically at eye level with my crotch—a serious power move. Placing an elbow on each knee, I cocked my head to the side and shouted, "What?"

Fumbling with the lace that framed the neck of her shirt, she looked down and said, "Um... you gonna go down the slide?"

"No, but you can sit up here with me," I said. I was not going to let go of that upper hand.

"Um, okay," said Tina. She clambered up the steps and wedged herself between the safety guard and me. At that moment, a brilliant idea struck me.

"Dare you to bite me," I said.

Tina stared at me, equally confused and terrified. "No way!" she said, anxiously readjusting herself atop the slide.

"Just do it... bite me." I was doing my best to keep a cool demeanour.

"No... you're gonna tell on me."

"C'mon. I won't tell. Just bite me."

Tina didn't move. "You will. You'll tell on me."

This exchange went on for several minutes, my desperation growing as we continued to dominate the slide. I was so eager for her to indulge my bizarre request to sink her teeth into my anemic, freckled skin.

"Tina... Just bite me. I am *not* going to tell, I *promise.*"

Her eyes widened. "You promise?"

There it was. The promise. This one word was all I needed to gain her trust. She may have been misguided, but a promise meant something to four-year-old Tina. From my perspective, though, a promise was more of a loose

"Dare you to bite me,"
I said. Tina stared
at me, equally
confused and terrified.
"No way!"

commitment, easily instantly disregarded, like when your twenty-two-year-old mom receives an invitation to go water skiing with her friends the same weekend you had planned a bike ride together.

I looked deep into her innocent, mud-coloured eyes and swore, "I *pinky* promise."

After an apprehensive moment, Tina took my arm and softly wrapped her hands around my bony wrist. Her nails were clean against my skin—she hadn't yet experienced the pleasure of digging deep enough into the sandbox to reach where the cool underlay of clay meets your fingertips. My own nails were jagged, with unidentified crud securely rooted in my nail beds.

She bit down on me, hard—really hard—breaking my delicate, chalky skin and leaving a significant enough indentation that a dentist could have made a mould of her baby teeth off my tender arm.

She had gone too far. My fantasy of a seductive, lovely nip had turned into something that might require a rabies vaccine.

I immediately climbed off the slide, ran to the nearest adult, and told on her.

Sweet revenge. This will teach her not to fuck with me. Bossy? Pffft.

As the teachers dragged her into the administration office, I heard her crying in desperation, "She told me to! She made me do it!" Of course, no one believed her. While I *was* rather wild, no one thought I could be sinister or strategic enough to coerce another child into biting me. The idea was absolutely absurd—ill-behaved children *do* the biting, they don't ask to be bitten.

Tina, if you're reading this, I was clearly deeply disturbed. You were baited into a trap that served no other purpose than to quell my deep insecurity about having to share you with other friends. I was also a bossy little shit who very soon had to learn how to temper my imperious nature. Please email me at sorry@notthatlikeable.com if you'd like to share your own version of this story, receive an apology, or tell me that this biting incident was the catalyst for joining the BDSM community. You do you, boo. Oh, and tell your friends about my book, because this bird is a biter.

TYLER THE GARBAGE MAN

"I can see the rainbow.
I like jelly in the bowl.
I am six."

AMANDA, age six, having deep revelations

MY FLAIR FOR THEATRICS, especially when it involved an indulgent temper tantrum, meant I never made drop-off a breeze for my mother. Early each morning, she would dump me at daycare and, without fail, I would holler, shed my weight in tears, and pound on the greasy windows that imprisoned me in preschool hell. Perhaps not coincidentally, around this same time, my mom and I went to go live with my grandparents.

At twenty-two, my mom was working double shifts, often overnight, at a nursing facility not far from my grandparents' home. I don't have children of my own and I am not nearly under the same kind of pressure she was, but there have still been occasions when I myself have unapologetically considered dumping my friends' kids off on the side of the highway. (There are only so many times in one five-minute stretch that one can tolerate hearing "I'm so hungry!" after someone's crotch spawn has turned their nose up at what was yesterday's favourite snack. *Goldfish are fucking great, you koala-sized asshat.* Now *that's* a title for a children's book I want to write.) My mother is a natural empath, generous and patient, and the only person I know who can literally clean up other people's shit without losing her mind. She has devoted her career and life to supporting marginalized people, from the abandoned seniors she assisted early in her career to the work she continues to do as a teacher's aide for children with diverse physical disabilities and learning challenges. I admire my mom as she naturally stepped into the role of caretaker to help my grandparents with errands and little chores around the house—bitching about it only 99 percent of the time.

So, my remaining trips to daycare started at my grandparents' house. While I mostly hated the whole daycare experience, I fucking loved the crafts. Early on, I showed promise in the arts, and it became an opportunity for me to flaunt my talents to anyone who cared to acknowledge my mad scissor skills. There were also a lot of snacks and I love snacks, especially since daycare provided me with exotic treats I had never seen before, like Ants on a Log (celery with peanut butter and raisins) and carrots and dip (aka toddler's crudités). These delicacies were a far cry from the boxes of Smarties I hid between the unmade sheets of my twin bed.

One of my favourite activities included colouring Styrofoam cups with crayons, placing them in the oven on low heat and watching them melt into nameless shapes. After "cooking," the teacher would present us with these colourful blobs of joy and I would return home, proudly holding my creation (or, rather, my cremation) up to my grandfather's belly, allowing him to take in the cheerful mound of toxic carcinogens.

Another visceral memory includes the smell of Plasticine. As soon as that putty-coloured material was slapped in front of me, I modelled the shit out of my next masterpiece, taking in the olfactory sensations like a crafting addict. Much to my disappointment, all of my modelling "skillz" went to waste and the Oscars never did come calling for my one-frame stop-motion film.

At some point, the daycare underwent a renovation to add two toilets inside the actual classroom. I suspect this was done so that our considerably underpaid teachers (read: babysitters) didn't have to lug our blowouts down the hall when we couldn't make it to the bathroom in time. One day, right after the new washrooms had reached completion, we were filed into two lines for a "pre-nap pee" followed by a quick brush of our teeth. Imagine it: one large, open room with two sinks and two toilets and no partitions. Was this a construction deficiency? Did the general contractor know about this missing scope of work? For the record, I've squatted over shallow holes carved out of the earth with only a plastic shower curtain and sign translating to "No Poop" that had more privacy. As my short legs dangled from the cool toilet, midstream, I looked up at the row of nitwits in line to pee after me and then to my left at a boy also popping a squat on the adjacent toilet. I was absolutely mortified and did not understand why we had been forced to do our business in front of all our classmates. I swathed a sizable wad of toilet paper—an amount that would have had my grandfather simultaneously cursing all the women in our family as he plunged the toilet—and wiped, in the wrong direction (a fact that I wouldn't learn until I was in my early thirties on a camping trip with friends who clearly had parents who cared about the hygiene of their children's yonis). Flushing the toilet, I pulled up my soft pink corduroy pants and went to the sink to brush my teeth—which was strangely close to the toilet, leaving our toothbrushes, also next to the sink, fully vulnerable to the fecal matter that was likely spraying up only a few inches away. As I searched for my toothbrush, Tyler, who was next in line to use the toilet, pointed at the trash bin. I looked down and saw my toothbrush jammed between wads of snotty toddler tissue.

Tyler stared at me dumbly and said, "I'm a garbage man," and then made some sort of inimitable noises that sounded like a Tiësto mix of guns and exhaust—you know, the types of sounds that only boys can make. "Pew-pew-pew-pew-pew."

"Scuse me, Tyler… why is my toothbrush in the garbage?"

"Vvvrrrooommm." Tyler spun his hands around an imaginary steering wheel. "I threw out your toothbrush because I'm a garbage man!"

What. Is. This. Fuckery.

I recognized that Tyler had very likely been gifted with the IQ of an overly steamed turnip, all of his grey matter being extracted of its nutrients during childbirth, and I imagined ramming my toothbrush into his ear canal in such a manner that, at pick-up time, his parents would think he was wearing one of those novelty prank head-injury Halloween headpieces. I was taller than Tyler *and* three months older. I placed one hand on my hip, leaned in, and said, "Whyyy'd you do that?"

"I'm a garbage man! I threw it in the trash! Vrooommm." Tyler bopped around, lost in his own waste-filled world, imagining the day when he would be promoted to director of sanitation. Tyler's parents were likely the type of people who said things like, "YOU CAN BE ANYTHING YOU WANT, TYLER! IF YOU BELIEVE IT, YOU CAN BECOME IT!" I've always enjoyed imagining the lives of others, and Tyler's was no exception.

Tyler's dad arrives home each day at 5:10 p.m. after a short commute from his office job on the outskirts of downtown, in a practical but stylish car—a Ford Escort. Ceremoniously, he places his briefcase atop the console in the front entry. The worn leather of this hand-me-down previously belonged to Tyler's grandfather, who had owned a modest insurance company. Tyler's father had never risen to the occasion of taking over the family business and, during the holidays, this fact remained obviously exhumed like a deceased family pet who is occasionally vulnerable to being dug up. Tyler's father tempered the bones of this familial disappointment with fanatical enthusiasm about his son's desire to collect trash.

Tyler's mother prepares dinner each night. Each morning, she heaves open her copy of The Joy of Cooking, *which was gifted to her by her mother-in-law, thus impressing upon her the importance of being a "good wife." Anticipating the hunger and palate of her boys, she labours over a meal that is shared with a side of congenial conversation centred on Tyler's fascinating adventures at daycare.*

"Teacher! Teacher! Tyler threw out my toothbrush!" I screamed. As we have learned, I was not above telling on anyone.

Exhausted, my teacher returned my frantic cries for justice with an "*Oh, Amanda.*" Patronizing is the worst kind of response for a kid growing up in a weird extended family who already struggles with a strained sense of belonging.

"It was *obviously* an accident. Tyler wouldn't throw your toothbrush out."

Tyler's smug eyes met mine and the corners of his mouth distinctively moved into a smirk. Psychotic little prick—not as stupid as he looked, after all.

"But—" I started in, only to be told "Nap time!" This injustice precipitated my belief that I was living in a dystopian reality where I'd become the antagonist. I had six adults to whom I had to explain my behaviour and I never knew which one was going to take my side.

Flopping down on the gym mat that made for our make-shift nap station, I curled up on my side, my back turned to both Tyler and my teacher to hide my sulky face. As I fell asleep, I thought about vindicating my claims against this burgeoning garbage man by stealing all of the kids' tooth-brushes so that Tyler would finally get what was coming to him. No sooner had I worked out my plan than I drifted into a deep sleep, transporting myself to the dinner table at Tyler's house, taking in the smells of roast ham, glazed carrots, and the subtle scent of bleach in the kitchen.

Tyler, I really do hope you fulfilled your dream of becoming a garbage man. Holla at your girl (sorry@notthatlikeable .com), as I wouldn't mind a replacement toothbrush. Soft bristled, thanks.

HOW TO
SELL WATER

"Dear Tooth Fairy, Sorry I lost my tooth. I believe in you! All give you my tooth if I find it. Please can you leave something." Love Amanda

AMANDA, age six or so, hopeful

WITH THE EXCEPTION of my uncle David, everyone in my family worked for the education system. My grandmother, who has her master's degree in education, always ensured that I had the best books on hand—you know, not the ones that you actually wanted to read, but the ones that had those big gold-foil Caldecott Medal stickers. She was also the killjoy who censored my opportunity to watch mind-numbing shows like *Pee-wee's Playhouse*, which was probably a good thing because I think Pee-wee ended up showing his "wee-wee" in an adult theatre years later. Grandma knows best.

Even before I was of school age, I had a growing collection of metaphor-heavy, adult-approved books. So, I decided to launch my first business, which really ended up being more of a community project. I took it upon myself to share the wealth of knowledge that I had amassed through critical literature like *The Velveteen Rabbit*, *Where the Wild Things Are*, and *The Owl and the Pussycat*. I went through the painful task of creating individual envelopes and insert slips so that I could sign books out and catalogue my growing inventory. Word on the street was that I had a good thing going, but since my grandparents wouldn't let me invite strangers over, my only customers were the two girls who lived across the road: Andrea and her neighbour Meaghan. My basement library may never have met its full potential, but it gave me the hope of someday having enough money to buy all of the five-cent candies one could ever want—and so have plenty of bait for engaging the neighbourhood kids.

That wasn't my last attempt at commerce. Late in the summer, I tended to go a bit stir-crazy, and my experimentation with different "business models" would become more than a little bizarre. Our garage—a detached one-vehicle deal that had a front-facing drive—was, in effect, a junk warehouse, which made it a goldmine of miscellaneous props, tools, and other shit that allowed my imagination to run wild. To this day, that garage has never actually seen a vehicle. My grandparents keep it as more of a storage locker, where outdated paperwork—some of which predates the '80s—goes to die. (I suspect they both thought that if shit ever went sideways or the apocalypse came, those countless reams of paper would come in handy for starting a bonfire. I don't fault them for planning for the future, and, after all, that hoarding meant my diaries were preserved, which made this book possible.) One of my favourite games was to use all that junk to design an obstacle course in the front yard. On any given day, it might consist of old tires, lengths of rope and chain, expanses of fishing net, and lobster traps. The local kids would mostly just ride their bikes by and laugh—making it a bit of a flop as a business idea—but Andrea and I would time each other as we raced to the finish line. She'd also agree to let me strap her into a hand truck and sprint her down the street. Eventually, we'd tire of these antics and return to terrorizing the neighbourhood like punks on our butterfly-covered bikes, blowing through stop signs and unmarked intersections, and basically giving every driver in the area a near heart attack.

After one such neighbourhood jaunt, I decided to truly monetize my endless ideas by opening a lemonade stand. While I could barely spell my own name, it didn't stop me from seeking out capital to invest in Candy Futures on the TSX. Those days, like now, I woke up naturally before 5 a.m., because that's what successful businesspeople do. (As an adult, I still tell myself this story—and I say the same thing to friends when I announce my morning rise time to them. Yet another attempt to cull my deep sense of inadequacy.) On the morning of my lemonade-stand idea, fully invigorated by candy-fuelled calories and tenacity, I hauled an antique side table from our living room out onto the front porch. I was confident that my product would be so good that I wouldn't need to find a busy sidewalk corner. Word would get around; my customers would come to me.

A naturally gifted artist, I free-handed a sign that strategically communicated, through typeface and brand identity, that my lemonade was the best in all the land. Now that my brick-and-mortar space was ready for occupancy, it was time to make my product. There was just one very small detail: the lemonade.

I searched through the freezer for frozen mix but came up empty. I thought perhaps there might be some powdered mix in the pantry. Nope. The more I thought about it, the more I realized that I couldn't actually remember ever drinking lemonade at home.

After some consideration, I realized that this oversight on my part was a blessing in disguise. After all, no self-respecting entrepreneur serves pre-made lemonade to her patrons. I opted to make the lemonade from scratch. That would show the true integrity behind my brand.

I ran outside and added "homemade" to my lemonade sign, then went back in the house and gathered the necessary tools: a pitcher, a cutting board, a butter knife, some sugar, and a few lemons. Wait, where are the lemons?! Dammit, Amanda.

Quickly pivoting my business plan, I returned to the freezer and rifled through it for a can of orange juice: Minute Maid, not from concentrate, with pulp. Frostbitten bags of peas and corn left over from holidays past and Ziploc bags filled with perogies dominated the shelves. We always had orange juice. Except, of course, this one time, when I needed it most.

With fewer than a dozen years on earth, my business brain kicked into high gear. "Come on…" I muttered into the freezer, the cool air spilling out and chilling my uncovered legs. "Ya gotta be kidding me!"

It was nearing 7 a.m. and it was imperative that I capture the early rush. So, in a last-ditch effort to salvage my plan, I settled for a jug of lukewarm tap water. Spilling the water along the way, I shuffled as quickly as possible back to my "store" and was dumbfounded to see that no one had yet lined up for a glass.

After an hour, and just as I was losing hope, our letter carrier came wandering down the street. Despite being early, it was already quite hot. I had already indulged in my own stash of bathwater while I was waiting, and I thought that, surely, she too would want a glass. As the mail carrier approached the house, I stood up, angling my bony hips off to the left, with one hand on my waist and the other holding the jug.

"Lemonade?" she asked. Putting down her bag, she said, "But I don't have twenty-five cents! Will you take ten cents?"

I didn't have the heart to tell her that it was water. "I made it fresh this morning," I said instead. At this point, the mail carrier was distracted, simultaneously shuffling through her bag for our mail and a dime. I took the opportunity to swiftly pour her a glass and push it towards her.

I didn't have the heart to tell her that it was water. "I made it fresh this morning," I said instead.

She gulped down some "lemonade," her face turning as she realized she had been duped—this was not a chilled glass of citrus juice.

As was my habit with all adults, I looked up at her and anxiously awaited her approval. "So?" I asked.

Nodding, she gave me an apprehensive, "Um... thanks. Yes, very good." She gently placed the dime and her mostly full glass of water back onto the table. Passing me our mail, she stepped down from the porch, kindly waving goodbye as she walked off. And, like the good shopkeeper I was, I called out, "Thank you! Please come again!"

6

LIKE A VIRGIN

"I love to read! School is very fun! I have blue eyes! Me and my mom are weird sometimes! In the summer I say 'there's my crazy mother' but she didn't say anything. Me and my mom always call each other funny names. Like I call her sometimes Memop. She sometimes calls me pumpkin, when she is happy."

AMANDA, Grade 1 diary entry

ONE MORNING before daycare, I put on my favourite jean skirt. The body of the skirt was adorned with ruffled denim fabric and the waist was capped with an elastic band. The skirt was now too small, so I had to hike it up higher on my waist, making it unbearably short and tight—and my mom knew it. But I loved it anyway, because it allowed me to channel my inner Madonna, an unusual idol for someone who still wet the bed from time to time.

While other little girls were idolizing Barbie, I loved the Queen of Pop. My mom had a cool collection of cassette tapes, and we would bop around to *Like a Virgin*. I'd toss my head of curls, held back by a velvet hairband, and she'd lip-sync the words to all the songs. While Madonna might not have been the most appropriate icon for a preschooler, I could still recognize her give-no-shits attitude and wanted to manifest that same confidence. She was the embodiment of cool.

"Put some panties on," croaked the Deb. She sounded like she had been smoking cigarettes with Loretta, her favourite emphysema resident at the nursing home, after a split-shift bender of dirty adult diapers. While she turned a blind eye to the too-short skirt, she didn't need my ass making an appearance on our brisk walk to school.

"No. Don't wanna," I blurted.

"Amanda Marie—"

"No! I don't wanna!"

"Don'tcha take that tone of voice with me, missy," spat the Deb in my direction. The freckles scattered across her face seemed to lose colour against her burning cheeks. In retrospect, I can see that she probably hadn't slept much and the last thing she wanted to do was manage my attitude problem. Among my six parents, I'm not sure who she thought she was, and I was annoyed that her part-time mothering meant full-time bossing me around. But she scared me when she got angry, so I caved and put on underwear.

As soon as I got to daycare, I balled up my panties and tucked them into my My Little Pony backpack. By the afternoon, I had completely forgotten that I was going au naturel, and that's when our teacher had us all sit around in a circle, cross-legged. Things were feeling pretty breezy.

For some reason, my mom showed up early and was talking to one of the teachers at the emergency door at the back of the classroom. I thought it odd but paid her no attention and went back to watching one of the kids methodically circle the group, patting each head with a "Duck." Just as the kid's hand was about to reach me (*Goose, goose*, I whispered to myself), my mother grabbed my elbow and tore me from the circle.

"Heyyy!" I shouted.

"Amanda. Where. Are. Your. Panties?" she hissed. The Deb was rather upset. I was scared. Cautiously, I pointed at the backpack she was holding in the hand that wasn't death-gripping my elbow. Releasing her hold on me, she opened the front pocket to discover my floral ginch stashed next to a deflated juice box. Exasperated, she closed the zipper and stared at me.

"You're not gonna make me put them back on?" I asked.

"Amanda. Where. Are. Your. Panties?" she hissed. The Deb was rather upset.

Noticeably exhausted, she sighed, and said, "No." With her free hand, she clasped mine and we walked home in silence. Looking up at her, I wondered if she still loved me after I had, as she would say, pulled another one of my "stunts." I thought about how cool she was and how proud Madonna would have been of us at that very moment. I suspect none of us was wearing panties.

7

STUFFED
IN A SOFA

"This is a window. I love windows."

AMANDA, age five, easily pleased

I'VE BEEN TOLD this story many times and, while I remember all the details of it, it's always funny to hear my aunt Karen and uncle Bobby argue over who showed up for me more that day. Karen had what might be considered among intellectuals a borderline unhealthy obsession with collecting horse figurines, so, truthfully, I'm not entirely sure about the validity of any of these details. In typical fashion, this story, like many others in our family, hides like missing Brothers Grimm folklore alongside the reams of scholastic papers and dated slides buried within the archives of what was once a functional garage at my grandparents' home.

On Friday, July 31, 1987 (forever known to locals as Black Friday), a seriously gnarly tornado ripped through Edmonton. Starting in the southeast area of the city, the funnel remained on the ground for just over an hour and left a path of destruction for almost thirty-one kilometres. It reached its maximum intensity, an F4 on the Fujita scale, just one kilometre from our family home, in an area called Refinery Row. Hucking hail larger than tennis balls, the tornado tossed around oil tanks and levelled several industrial buildings. And it wasn't alone: a total of six tornadoes touched down in and around Edmonton that day.

What do I remember? Being stuffed in a sofa.

1:40 p.m.: *Severe Weather Watch issued.* The teachers at Peter Pan Child Care Centre listen nervously to the radio.

2:45 p.m.: *Severe Weather Warning issued.* The teachers begin contacting parents. They make several attempts to reach someone at my home but are unsuccessful.

3:04 p.m.: *Tornado Warning issued.* With ominous funnel clouds quickly approaching at her back, my aunt Karen leaves the shelter of her desk at the *Edmonton Sun* newspaper facility and races home on her pedal bike, worried that her beloved niece is going to get swept away in a *Wizard of Oz*–esque funnel. Before leaving, she manages to get hold of my uncle Bobby and gets him to pick me up at daycare.

3:25 p.m.: *Tornado causes F2 to F3 damage in Southeast Edmonton.* Aunt Karen reaches home, frantic. "Amanda, get downstairs!" she shouts. (Like my grandmother, she tends to worry a lot, but this also makes her responsible. She knows how to take charge.) I am standing at the window in our dining room with Uncle Bobby. The sky above the backyard is moody and majestic, with mossy undertones that transition to hickory and then aubergine.

"Whoaaa. That's so cool!" I shout, pointing at the sky.

"Would ya look at that!" he responds.

I stand on tiptoe to look out the window, my nose resting on the sill. Uncle Bobby, who is a bit of a science nerd, is fascinated.

"Here," he says, pulling over a dining chair so I can better see outside. "Look at the colour of the sky. Pretty neat, hey?"

"Bobby!" Aunt Karen yells. "We need to get downstairs. The news is saying we need to be in the basement." I'm torn between which pseudo-parent I'm supposed to be following. *Where is my mom?* I think. I've forgotten that she left earlier that day to meet some friends at the lake for the weekend. My grandparents are also out of town, sailing on the *Godolphin* with my uncle David.

"Come, Uncle Bobby!" I say. I figure I can appease them both by appealing to each of their needs. Obediently, I follow my aunt into the basement (or, as we called it, the rumpus room) while gesturing to my uncle to follow. One look at my needy outstretched arm and he caves, grabbing my hand and following us into the basement.

"I think she should get under the piano," Aunt Karen states. Uncle Bobby thinks that's silly, and the two of them get into a debate about the best location to protect their niece. Ignoring them, I plunk myself down on the piano bench and strain to reach the pedals. It's a player piano, and as my feet pump away, the perforated roll of music advances and ragtime echoes from its belly. My hands float above the keys, bobbing rhythmically to a steady bass line. (Soon, this same piano seat will be shared with Andrea as we pretend to play duets together to music we don't understand.)

"Amanda, get underneath the piano," Aunt Karen directs.

"But why? What's the piano gonna do?" I ask. I'm genuinely curious.

Uncle Bobby rolls his eyes and jumps on the back of the sofa to peer out the basement window. I scramble towards him and climb up the back of the sofa. Cupping me under my arms, Bobby holds me up to look outside the basement window.

"The recommendation was to hide in the basement, under something sturdy," Aunt Karen says.

"Yeah, like a table," Uncle Bobby scoffs. "Not a piano. What if that thing falls on her?"

"Well, where should she go, then?" my aunt asks.

I jump off the sofa and wander around the basement, looking for something fun to do. "I'm bored. Can we go back upstairs and look out the big window?"

"You want to stuff Amanda in the sofa?" says Uncle Bobby. "Well, what else do you suggest?" Karen responds.

"Yeah, Karen, can't we go back upstairs and look out the window?" Uncle Bobby mimics.

I join him on the back of the sofa again, but the view just isn't as good as it would be upstairs—all I can see are the untended weeds along the perimeter of the house. Aunt Karen has the radio blaring, waiting for instructions.

3:30 p.m.: *Tornado reaches peak intensity. F4 damage created just blocks from our house at Refinery Row.*

"This thing is coming right for us," Aunt Karen says. "We need to take shelter. Let's move that sofa away from the windows and outside walls and get Amanda in it."

"You want to stuff Amanda in the sofa?" says Uncle Bobby.

"Well, what else do you suggest? This way she is protected from anything falling over on her," Karen responds.

Bobby and Karen pick up the sofa and move it away from the window, placing it along an interior wall. Lifting up the faux velvet seats, my aunt directs me to lie down, and then layers the cushions over me, my face poking out between them like a baby crowning.

"Why'm I under here?" I ask. I still don't understand the level of destruction amassing just a quick bike ride away.

Aunt Karen ignores me while Uncle Bobby pretends to sit on the sofa and I giggle amid the dusty foam. For about thirty or forty minutes we remain like this, listening to the news and waiting for either the house to crumble or the tornado to pass.

4:25 p.m.: *Tornado moves across Edmonton. A nearby community is hit with F2 to F3 damage.*

OF COURSE, every time we tell this story, my mom butts in, insisting she was there. She was not. I don't remember crying or being afraid, but looking back on this now, I recognize how terrifying it must have been for my young aunt and uncle as they assumed full responsibility for me. Both had only recently graduated from high school and were probably keen to use the house to party while their parents were out of town. Instead, they had a five-year-old to tend to, one who felt to them like a much younger sibling rather than a niece.

When I returned to kindergarten the following Monday, and for years following, I told my peers that the tornado had ripped off the corner of our roof and we had narrowly escaped danger. It became another expression of my early attention-seeking behaviour, as I used this wildly exaggerated "fact" to lure impressionable kids into conversation with the hopes of garnering friendships. Sometimes it worked, and other times, especially when I tried the tactic on kids who were more emotionally secure, they would see right through my bullshit. I've always felt bad about using this bold-faced lie, but I understand now that for every story, there are multiple truths, and no single version is ever 100 percent accurate. Our individual experiences shape parts of our history that become real for us, even if it means that, over time, the stories evolve, becoming fables of our muddled past. Later, these stories can turn into limiting beliefs, trauma we need to recover from, or, in this case, simply an understanding that sometimes we tell our own version as a way to survive or thrive. These are simply the stories we tell ourselves.

To those impressionable children I deceived, you know where to reach me. ✌

8

TUESDAY'S PANTIES

"I'm going to take a shit! Kiss ass!"

MY BABY BOOK, in my mom's handwriting.
Then, underneath: "Amanda, age four"

FROM CHILDHOOD through my adult years and right up to today, no number of fecal tests, digestive enzymes, probiotics, and elimination diets, and no amount of complaining, or changing my last name to "Hamilton" (which does have a much better sounding pedigree), has saved me from the Whelan Family Guts. On a genetic level, we just can't trust our guts... and I'm not talking here about the instinct sense of the phrase—in terms of intuition—I mean this quite literally. As someone with self-diagnosed IBS-D, "trusting my gut" typically does not work out in my favour.

I'd like to say I've solved the problem by avoiding cramp-inducing meals, but no matter what I eat, there seems to be no end to the varied responses of my digestive system. I'm convinced that my gut has some kind of personality disorder with manic tendencies. According to the internet, which is 100 percent accurate at all times, these are the eight symptoms of borderline personality disorder, and my IBS-D checks all of them:

☑ **Fear of Abandonment.** With my fast metabolism, my stomach is hungry and needy for caloric intake at all times.

☑ **Unstable Relationships.** Including, but not limited to, dairy sensitivity, gluten intolerance, soy sauce allergy, and a revolt against some weird ingredient called carrageenan. Doesn't like sugar, most nuts, corn, fibre, or any gluten alternatives. Hates yeast.

☑ **Unclear or Shifting Self-Image.** My stomach alters from being barren and sexless to being the size of a thirteen-month pregnancy after any meal. Waist size unknown. Pre-meal jean size 26/27. Post-meal jean size, unzipped with my gut hanging out in a semi-reclined position.

☑ **Impulsive, Self-Destructive Behaviours.** Cravings include McDonald's Happy Meals at 11 p.m., Mama Burgers with cheese, high-quality butter carried into my gaping yap by warm, freshly baked sourdough bread, and mega-pints of red wine.

☑ **Self-Harm.** Consumption of aforementioned cravings.

☑ **Extreme Emotional Swings.** Chill, cool, relaxed tummy one moment, and in the next, angry, agitated, and volatile.

☑ **Chronic Feelings of Emptiness.** With streamlined "evacuation" procedures and the schedule of an entrepreneur.

☑ **Explosive Anger.** Explosive Diaheria. Dieheryeha. Diarehhera. Diereya. Dhieria. DIE-YER-E-HA. Oh, for fuck's sake, does anyone know how to spell this? DIARRHEA.

As an adult, I have learned to live with my unpredictable, high-maintenance body in the same way the owner of a classic car might get used to always having to make repairs. But when I was a kid, having to live under the constant threat of a poop attack was, well, less than ideal.

On one particular day, when I was in Grade 2, I was hanging out after school in the computer lab. (Being the principal's granddaughter had a few perks, like being able to have run of the halls after hours while I waited for Grandma to finish up and take me home. Despite hating math and being told that math hated me, I spent a lot of time in the computer lab playing *Number Munchers* and dying from dysentery in *Oregon Trail* on the school's Apple IIe, impatiently switching out the floppy disks between rounds. (Any teachers who saw me—usually delirious from prepping their lesson plans and/ or trying to impress "Mrs. Whelan"—would say I was "so patient waiting for Grandma," but I was actually bordering on being a computer game addict.) I suddenly needed to go, but as I was on my way to the washroom, shoes off and sock-sliding, I was distracted by an opportunity to converse with Mr. B, the school counsellor, of whom I was rather fond.

"Heyo, Mr. B," I said casually, making sure he saw a patient little girl. I had appearances to keep up.

"Well helllooowww, there! How is my Amanda?" His smile showcased the subtle gap between his two front teeth as his blue-grey eyes lit up.

I beamed. This was my time to shine! The washroom could wait.

"I really like playing *Oregon Trail*. But I don't really like the hunting part and my oxen are sick. My brother died of chowleruh. What's chowleruh?"

"It's pronounced caa-lr-uh," he answered. Just as Mr. B was about to explain what cholera was, a wave came over my body and I knew I needed to boogie to the girl's bathroom.

"'Kay bye, Mr. B. Gotta run!" I spun on my socked heel and shimmied, close-cheeked, like a power walker into the washroom. Without knowing it, I was about to have my own bout of cholera. Unfortunately, my conversation with Mr. B resulted in me being about 0.000001 seconds short of making it to the toilet before I shit myself in my overpriced pink corduroys.

"Uggghhh." I looked over at a stainless steel bin mounted to the partition and considered ditching my poo-filled panties. As I went to remove them, I saw, displayed on the crotch, a perky Care Bear holding the word "Tuesday" above her head. It was Thursday... was I still wearing Tuesday's panties? I couldn't throw that cute little bear in the garbage, not with her cheerful face looking at me. I got a wad of toilet paper and worked at cleaning the poo out of my underwear until I felt confident that I could pull Tuesday Bear back up over my bottom and face the world.

As I left the washroom, I heard my name come over the intercom—I was being called back to the principal's office. Andrea's dad, Mr. H, who also taught at the school, was my ride home that day and he was waiting for me with my backpack and shoes in hand.

"Ready to-to go?" Mr. H stuttered. He had a slight speech impediment, which I always thought was sort of neat and different.

"Yup! Let's boogie!" I anxiously grabbed my gear and ran ahead of him, my poopy stench likely wafting behind me as I beat him to his powder-blue Chevette. As soon as we got in the car, Mr. H immediately suggested we roll down the windows, saying it was a hot day. As we drove and chatted, I closed my eyes and tilted my head outside, enjoying the warmth of the sun against my face as I let my arm surf the breeze. I now realize that it was probably just a moderately warm day, and Mr. H was doing his very best to air out the vehicle so as not to succumb to a fecal-induced coma. Mr. H, I am very sorry. Please email me for a formal apology at sorry@notthatlikeable.com.

BRB. Gotta go poop. Like, for real.

9

SUNDAYS WITH ANDREA

"A sunny day
the clouds blauds
though the sun
i was lonelly."

AMANDA, age eight, navel-gazing

IT WAS A LAZY summer day, a dog day. The Deb was freshly greased with tanning oil that glistened provocatively against the loud neon print of her bikini, underwire and sympathetically placed ruching confidently masking the breasts of a woman ravaged years prior by a milk-thirsty child. In her delicate fingers with expertly polished acrylic nails, a du Maurier waited for its next acquaintance with her lips. These hands also held the stories of her life: inked on the outside of her left pinky finger was a butterfly; another decorated her equally delicate wrist. I watched her, clumsily mimicking her movements as she stylishly crossed her long limbs and slowly lifted her cigarette for its next inhale.

She turned to me, her hazel eyes piercing my own, and sweetly crooned, "Pumpkin—go run to the store and grab Mama some smokes." (She actually used a different word—a common British slang word for cigarettes that carries a very different meeting and shock level on this side of the pond. At the time, I assumed it was another sailing reference imprinted on my mother via my grandfather's "colourful" lingual inventory.)

I looked down at my own translucent skin, comparing its fair complexion to my mom's deep bronze.

"Why's your skin so brown an' mine's so white?" I inquired. Disregarding warnings of melanoma and UV skin damage, she slathered more oil on her body and tossed the slippery plastic container at me. It read: Hawaiian Tropic.

I turned the bottle over in my hands, trying to make out the ingredients. "What's am-ull ass-e-tait?"

The lids of my mom's closed eyes flickered open just a touch against the glare of the sun. She always refused to wear sunglasses—she didn't want to get "raccoon eyes."

"How does this work? Does this colour your skin darker? Does it make it brown like yours? Will it do that for me?"

I dumped a pool of oil in my hand and started rubbing it up and down my bony limbs.

"How long till it starts to work?"

The Deb stayed reclined on her plastic lawn chair—one of those kinds that looked like it had been constructed of rejected seatbelts—and turned her head a bit towards mine, squinting her eyes.

"Mandy..." She sighed my name like she was expelling a demon. "You gonna go to the store or what?"

"Yeah, Mama. I'll go."

Bike rides to the store were one of my favourite errands because they made very-small me feel very grown up. The trick was to expertly negotiate how much change my mom would let me use to buy Fun Dip, Nerds, and Smarties.

The corner store in question was the last unit in a long strip mall of depressed retail shops that sat across from the playground. My frequent visits usually earned me a disapproving look as I dumped my bike on its side directly in front of the entrance. The store sold carcinogens directly to children, in chic packages that sat seamlessly alongside baggies of five-cent candies.

On this visit, the owner rang through my stash alongside my mom's cigarettes, as always, choosing not to comment on my typical caloric intake of glucose, fructose, galactose,

My dishevelled clothing, greasy bangs, and malnourished-looking frame likely added to the impression that I didn't eat real food.

sucrose, and maltose. My dishevelled clothing, greasy bangs—
which were always a touch too short or touch too long—and
malnourished-looking frame likely added to the impression
that I didn't eat real food.

"Five dollars and thirty-seven cents."

I exposed a grubby palm full of random change and lint,
and dumped the slippery coins on the counter. I resented the
shiny loonies, new on the block in 1987, because they were
heavier to carry around than a balled-up wad of one-dollar bills.

"There's only four seventy-eight here. You're short fifty-
nine cents."

I opened my baggie of five-cent candies and, with hands
that smelled like a pina colada, picked out twelve candies and
left them on the counter.

"You've touched those now. You have to buy them."

"Oh. Oops. 'Kay, I'll get you back next time." This strategy,
one I had likely employed before, landed me an extra dozen
candies at no additional cost. With the opaque plastic bag
holding my stash swinging from my handlebars, I eyed up
the park across the street—home to many of my childhood
adventures and once again calling me over. Returning home,
I dropped my bike into an outbreak of dandelions, flipped the
cigarettes at my mom, and ran towards the back gate.

"Where are you headed off to, missy?"

"Andrea's." My candy winnings in hand, I ran across the
alley towards Andrea's house to stir up some adventure.

THE PLOT OF LAND that housed the daycare I had previously
attended had two parks separated by a large stretch of grass
that often hosted evening and weekend sports. It also acted
as an impasse, keeping a safe distance between the "big kids
park" and the "little kids park." This long stretch of grass lives
on in the recurring dreams I have of my childhood exploits.
Despite having six caretakers, I was frequently free of adult

supervision and would spend much of my time exploring the neighbourhood with my very bestest friend, Andrea.

In stark contrast to my house, Andrea's residence epitomized the type of home one would envision for a nice, stable nuclear family. While Andrea's house was almost a mirror image of our own, it was bright and felt like the perfect set for a sitcom based in the early '60s. Freshly laundered clothing smelling of lavender sat at the foot of each child's bed, sheets expertly tucked in to evoke a safe claustrophobia each night. The bedrooms were all themed, too. Andrea's room—she was the youngest—was finished with rainbow wallpaper to suit her sunny personality; her sister, Kristen, had lemon-coloured walls with matching curtains; and her brother, Matthew, had an oversized room in the basement that was plastered with posters of Tiffany and Janet Jackson.

Pretty much every weekend, I would sleep over at Andrea's house. In fact, this happened so often that I suspect my family probably owes her parents a lot of rent and food money. I preferred staying over at her place because a) she had better snacks, b) she had more Barbies, and c) she had *fruit punch*. She also had a dollhouse that her parents had bought at the farmers market, and we would spend hours playing house with plastic dolls that represented unrealistic standards of beauty. (We both collected the special-edition Barbies, but Andrea would never take hers out of their boxes—I'd try to convince her, but it never worked. She knew what would likely happen if she did, because each time I got a new collector Barbie myself, I'd immediately tear open the package, and within hours, they'd have new haircuts and far more risqué outfits. Years later, the dollhouse, dolls, and everything else would be lost when Andrea's house burned to the ground in a fire. Pour one out for all those perfect, still-in-box Barbies. I wish you had each gotten a chance to try out at least one miniature sexy bustier before your fiery end.)

Never mind not putting "Baby" in the corner. Nobody was to put Baby in our Catholic bellies, either.

"I'm naming my Barbie Chloe," I would say when I got a new one. I always named my Barbies Chloe. It felt rich and sophisticated, something I was not.

"Well, I'm naming my Barbie Samantha," she'd say. Andrea always named her Barbies Samantha.

At this point, we would usually start arguing over whose turn it was to have their Barbie date Ken. We were always fighting over Ken because I didn't have one in my own collection. If we were in the *Archie* comics we both read avidly, Andrea would clearly be the raven-haired Veronica, and I would be Betty, the girl next door who didn't have quite the same allure and never won the boys (Archie, to be specific). When we'd tire of that battle, we'd just let our dolls scissor each other, having no idea what it all meant.

Post-Barbie indulgence, Andrea and I would finish off most sleepover nights by watching *Dirty Dancing*. We'd be as wide-eyed as "Baby" herself as we watched her walk into the club, precariously cradling a watermelon in her arms. Enamoured by her hot-and-cold romance with Johnny, we'd spend the rest of the evening crazy for Swayze, attempting to gyrate our hips to "Do You Love Me." To this day, I have no idea how or why we were allowed to watch that film at such an impressionable age—perhaps Andrea's parents were trying to send a not-so-subtle message about romance, love, and unprotected sex. Never mind not putting "Baby" in the corner. Nobody was to put Baby in our Catholic bellies, either.

While these evening adventures, which sometimes included Ouija board sessions, were memorable in and of themselves, I loved the mornings best. If it was a Saturday, Andrea and I would draft up menus for the rest of the family to put in their breakfast order. We rarely ever actually made those breakfasts because, no matter what we put on our menus, Andrea's mom, Colleen, would always throw together some waffles served with berries, whipped cream, and maple syrup. And juice. Oh my, *the juice.* There were always frozen cans of it in the freezer, and I *lived* for that shit. On more than a few occasions, Colleen (my fourth mom) had to put me on rations because I would literally drink through the family's entire supply for the week in one afternoon.

If it was a Sunday, I'd accompany Andrea and her family to church, where I would spend most of my time eyeballing her family so I would know what to do next. There was a lot of standing up, sitting down, standing up again, and then kneeling—time I mostly spent praying for more candy, attention from Mom, and endless supplies of juice. When it was time to accept communion (which I wasn't allowed to do), I sat solo in the pew and flipped through the heavy-bound songbooks, trying to memorize all of the lyrics to "Lamb of God."

When I wasn't pretending to be an obedient Catholic, I spent a lot of time with Andrea at the local pool, which was just a few blocks from our homes. Later, when we were older, we'd attend the teen swim and meet up with the other neighbourhood losers who, like us, didn't know a thing about stealing their parents' alcohol or smoking pot in the ravine. (Instead of stealing and actually *drinking* the mezcal that Andrea's dad would bring home from his travels to Mexico, Andrea and I would instead admire the little worm at the bottom of the bottle.)

Andrea was always the better swimmer. Her parents put her through the full course of lessons, and she eventually went on to obtain her lifeguard certification. My parents' approach was a little more "street-smart"—it amounted to one lesson: "Don't drown." Skilled swimmers run in our water-loving family. My great-grandfather was an avid scuba diver and my grandfather, now in his late eighties, still swims on the regular and has been a passionate sailor his entire life. My mother was a diver and on more than one occasion surprised Andrea and me at a public swimming pool by gathering

Three generations of Whelan men + *moi.*

her limbs up from her lounge chair and suddenly leaping into a backflip off the tallest diving board with no hesitation. My own approach was far scrappier. I took one lesson, did a terrible job at following the prescriptive instructions, and never took another class again.

Andrea was also a skilled figure skater, having taken lessons for the better part of her childhood. In the winter, we would spend hours at the outdoor rink that, like the pool, was just a stone's throw away. The free skating area was set next to a hockey rink, and I recall lying in bed listening to the echo of the pucks bouncing off the boards when the older boys hit up the rink in the late evenings. Andrea often attempted to teach me how to do crossovers and salchows, but I never got the hang of it and would just clunk around in circles in her hand-me-down skates while she impressed the hockey boys with her waltz jumps.

While my mother had formal training in cutting hair, my own hair was regularly referred to as a "rat's nest." Fine and stringy, my hair had a way of knotting together to form a net so that, if you looked closely enough, you'd see bits of gravel, twigs, and dry grass picked up and retained from our many adventures making outdoor forts in my wild, unmanicured backyard. (Once, in my early thirties, I asked my hairstylist if she could return my hair to its natural colour. She informed me that "they don't make dye in shitty field mouse brown.") In contrast, Andrea's thick chestnut hair lay flat in a perfect blunt cut above her shoulders, clean bangs neatly resting along her forehead. When we played around with crimping our hair—which happened often—Andrea always seemed to achieve a playful look suited for the Disney Channel, whereas I would have been listed in the credits as "Street Urchin 3."

My grandmother, who loved to shop, spoiled me with expensive corduroy pants and crisp blouses from the many overpriced children's boutiques that she frequented on the weekends. In return, I represented the good Whelan name by carelessly grinding chlorophyll into the knees and using the sleeves as a mobile napkin after gorging on my second helping of that day's salty McDonald's fries. While these designer threads were pretty, they weren't *cool*. Andrea had *cool* clothes. Trying to copy her look, I'd don a chunky headband, colour-changing T-shirt, bike shorts, and flip-flops. We just called them thongs, not knowing that this would later be something shoved up our asses for the rest of eternity in avoidance of the—gasp—*panty line*. (The HORROR!)

Despite my attempts to look as chic as she did with her early '90s side ponytail, the boys always, *always*, went for Andrea. While I consider myself quite stylish now, to this day the only guys who hit on me are the ones wearing the free Coors Light T-shirt they scored from the two-four they just crushed solo. In the words of my dear friend Rachelle, "I pity any guy who tries to pick you up. You're very intimidating." She was slightly intoxicated when she said this, but perhaps she wasn't entirely wrong. Or at least that's the story I tell myself.

10

THE FUCK INCIDENT

"You are one of the sweetest little girls I have ever taught. xxx ooo"

MRS. S, note added to Amanda's Grade 2 diary

MY GRADE 2 TEACHER, Mrs. S, was one of my favourites. She had all of the students keep daily diaries, and every morning when we returned to class, we would each get a note from her about what we had written. I have so many vivid memories from this year, including the time I knelt on a tack over the lunch hour and had to extract it from my kneecap.

One morning, during our journaling time, I was in full planning mode for my birthday, which was still six months away.

Mrs. S,

Today is Wednesday, October 18th, 1989. When it is my birthday, I am inviting all of your kids. My gram.ma can drive us to my house. It will be fun even if I am inviting boys. It will still be fun. We are going to Bowinkles probably, we always do. I am inviting Andrea, my best friend, Mr. Hs kid...

Just as I was about to launch into all of the full-blown details, Ryan, my desk mate, interrupted me.

"Want some?" Ryan was pouring a blob of Elmer's white glue onto the tip of his finger, licking, and repeating. I don't know if I had a crush on him and wanted to impress him, but I definitely know that I desperately wanted to fit in. So, I too began eating Elmer's white glue.

He put a dab of glue on my finger, and I studiously placed it in my mouth. "Mmmm... this tastes... good." It did not taste good. Ryan replenished my glue for a second helping. Taking the bottle from him, I reviewed the label: *non-toxic.* As I write this, I'm salivating like Pavlov's dog for another hit of Elmer's, despite now knowing it "may be harmful if swallowed."

Mrs. S kept a pet hamster, named Fuzzy, in her classroom, and she would let us take turns bringing him home over the weekends and holidays. Given that I was the principal's granddaughter, I'm quite sure that I got some preferential treatment in how often I was given that honour. Looking back on this now, I really feel for the hamster. As he was shipped around to various households, he was very likely manhandled by nefarious children when all he wanted was to get the poop dislodged from his hairy little butt and sleep in a pile of cotton and wood chips. PETA would be outraged. (After seeing that I could sustain a life other than my own, my parents bought me my own hamster. I loved Hammy, but he was a real dick, with sharp yellow teeth and a propensity for escaping his cage. When he died, I buried him in the flowerbed at the front of our house, which never actually housed flowers—it was more a dirt and weed feature. A few months later, out of morbid curiosity, I tried to dig him up, but he was gone. Weird.)

One day, just prior to the holidays, Mrs. S abruptly stopped us in the middle of a math lesson to "have a conversation."

"Okay, everyone. We are going to take a little break from math and talk about something important." We all looked at each other, nodding in unison at the shared opportunity to avoid figuring out if forty-two was an odd or even number.

Mrs. S launched in. "Does everyone know what you call a boy's private parts?"

I was 100 percent sure that a boy's private parts were called a "dick." Why else would you call someone a "dickweed"?

I imagine her now at home, sitting in the modest bungalow purchased with her beginner teacher salary right after she received a permanent contract. She's enjoying a glass of malbec, perhaps a bit too warm for her liking, while she discusses with her husband how to effortlessly merge in the sex ed curriculum that is now part of the school's mandate, despite the fact that some of her students (namely, me) are still shitting themselves.

My hand shot up. Of course, I knew. Every eight-year-old knows this and we aren't stupid and our parents would never lead us astray. And Santa is the real deal too.

Mrs. S did not pick me. She pointed to one of the boys instead. This kid had a snotty nose and a weird haircut, and clearly had not reached the same societal rank as my future glue-eating husband and me.

"Penis!" he shouted, perhaps a little too enthusiastically.

My hand shot up again to correct him. Despite me almost giving myself tennis elbow, Mrs. S ignored my trembling hand.

"Penis. That's correct, Matthew. Thank you."

Okay, what the bloody hell. Penis? No, no, *no*! That was all wrong. I was 100 percent sure that a boy's private parts were called a "dick." Why else would you call someone a "dickweed" on the playground? No one was saying "Hey you, penisweed— you suck balls!" I mean, really. (In case you're wondering, as I was, about the meaning of dickweed, according to *Urban Dictionary* online, it's "a completely self-absorbed, useless asshole with shit for brains.") I considered my options, which included reporting my teacher to my grandmother for her inaccurate curriculum and poor lesson planning.

"Okay, what do you call a girl's private parts?"

This time, I did not immediately raise my hand because I literally had *no* idea. *None.* A girl in our class, with highly coveted, lustrous black locks, quietly raised her hand. She never spoke much in class, but I remember being envious of her natural beauty and elegance and the ease with which she carried herself. I was awkward, hosted a menagerie of bruises, and my bangs were always in a greasy mess atop my forehead.

"Vagina," she said.

My idol clasped her hands on her desk. She didn't flinch. Even the best of us, as fully grown women, flinch saying *vagina.* Not because we don't love our yonis but because the word "vagina" is akin to depraved words like "smegma," "phlegm," and ... "discharge." (Many of us grew up referencing our privates as our vagina only to find out recently that we got it all wrong. *Vulva?* The word can't leave my lips without a grimace.)

This wasn't my only notable experience with the power of words that year. Mrs. S had a daughter, Maryanne, and because we were each born into faculty family, we both had free rein of the entire school property, which included the school library, computer room, cafeteria, and most of the classrooms. Our favourite was the kindergarten room, as it had a playhouse where we would roleplay and frequently leave the trash from all the bags of chips and ice cream that we helped ourselves to from the cafeteria.

One lunch hour on a Tuesday, Maryanne and I were fussing around in her mom's classroom and playing on the blackboard.

"What do you wanna do?" I asked her. Really, I was prompting her to ask the same so that I could direct our lunchtime activities to my liking.

"I dunno. What do you wanna do?" she responded. Match point.

"Let's play on the blackboard. I'll say words out loud, and you have to spell them right."

I kicked off the game right away by giving her the first word: "mountain." Obediently, she picked up a small piece of chalk and began to write on the board. Then, she gave me an equally benign word, "courage."

This went on for some time and I grew bored.

"I don't wanna play anymore," I said, and moved on to giving my attention to the hamster.

"'Kay. I'll wipe off the board," said Maryanne. She picked up the brush and erased our pseudo spelling bee.

"Come here!" I called. "Come see the hamster! Look at what he's doing!" I tapped at the bars of the cage, pointing to the hamster's butt up in the air as he burrowed into a nest he had made for himself.

I looked at Maryanne and said, "I have one more word."

I whispered it in her ear.

"Nuh-uh. That's a bad word. You'll tattle," she objected. But much like with Tina and the biting incident, I continued to work on coercing her.

"I'm the principal's granddaughter," I said. "We're not gonna get in trouble."

"What if we get caught?" she asked. She pulled at her shirt, and I noticed how her stringy, mouse-coloured hair looked much like mine. I wondered if maybe we were long-lost sisters, separated at birth. It would be super cool to have a sister.

"Not gonna happen, Maryanne."

"'Kay, but *you* have to write it."

Confidently, I strutted back to the board in a way that would make Madonna proud and selected a fresh piece of chalk. I put the chalk to the board and wrote the word out in giant capital letters:

FUCK

"See?" I said, turning around arrogantly to assure Maryanne that we wouldn't get in trouble. But she wasn't there. She had immediately bolted out of the classroom and ran straight into the lap of her mother, Mrs. S, where she promptly told on me.

As soon as I saw she was gone, I knew what was coming next. Frantic, I looked around for the brush to remove the evidence, but I couldn't find it anywhere. Maryanne was the last person to have it. I tried using the sleeve of my shirt, but that proved unsuccessful; the fine threads of the clothing provided absolutely no texture for removing the chalk.

Maryanne returned with her mother—my favourite teacher.

Remnants of "FUCK" remained on the blackboard.

I did what any kid would do: I told her a bold-faced lie.

"I didn't do it," I said. "Maryanne wrote that." Obviously, Maryanne objected, but I held firm. I believed she had intentionally hidden the chalk brush on me, and I wanted to get her back. *Bitch.*

Mrs. S led me and my chalked sleeves down to the principal's office. For most people, the principal's office is not a place of comfort. For me, it was a refuge where I could dump my backpack after school, kick off my stinky Velcro shoes, wrap my arms around my grandmother's generous waist, and bury my face into her large bosom. This time, however, Grandma's office was the home of an unrecognizably angry, red-faced, embarrassed woman who was about to suspend her own granddaughter.

I know. I *know.* At this point, you're probably thinking, *Amanda, you deserved this. This was payback for the biting incident.* And you're absolutely right.

My grandmother pulled me out of classes that afternoon and had me start my suspension in the library. The funny thing is, I *loved* the library. I was a bookworm and could be regularly found lost in *Alice in Wonderland, Where the Wild*

Things Are, or *The Lion, the Witch and the Wardrobe*. If reading books is punishment, then sign me up for a lifetime of
suspension!

The next day, I was told to stay home. My grandfather
had to take a day off work to watch me, and he was not happy
about it. I woke up early to find him sitting at the head of our
kitchen table—a spot usually reserved for my grandmother—
eating breakfast. As he spread marmalade over his lightly
toasted whole wheat bread, he looked at me seriously and
muttered, "I am very disappointed in you." My heart sank.

Disappointment. It's the worst. And to disappoint my
grandfather—a gentle-hearted soul who keeps a laid-back attitude about almost everything (perhaps with the exception of
how to execute a left-hand turn or any errand requests from
my grandmother, who is very specific about the type of cran-
berry sauce she wants)—cuts particularly deep. The parental
"disappointment" technique is a valuable tool, indeed. In fact,
paired with Catholic guilt, it's a nuclear weapon.

After returning from my suspension, the diary I kept with
my teacher every day changed from me telling stories to a
deep need to know I was "being good."

December 13, 1989

Amanda: I love you Mrs. S very much and I'm sorry what I did
to your Dother.

Mrs. S: It's OK, I love you too. We should think of things before
we do them. Remember your idea about counting to 10. Or,
we could make a mind picture of something warm and fuzzy
if we are mad.

December 19, 1989

Amanda: I love you Mrs. S. My mom made up with Leon 4 weeks
ago and I am glad. P.S. Do you love me too?

Mrs. S: I'm really glad you're glad. I love to see you happy. You sure have been happy lately. You have had one good smiley, happy day after another.

December 20, 1989
Amanda: I love you. Am I being good? P.S. Remember I will do good.

Mrs. S: You are being very good. Amanda, you don't have to always be good. Don't forget that we have the right to make a mistake.

January 9, 1990
Amanda: I love you! I haven't failed yet or skipped yet. When I get home, I am reading. Then I will get out a piece of paper and pencil and write you what I got. P.S. Do you love me?

Mrs. S: I sure do love you. I don't think you should think about failing and skipping. We should just think about doing our best at what we are doing right now.

Later, in my thirties, I found a diary that I had given my grandfather that was filled with prompts intended for him to complete. On one page, in answer to the question "What is one thing you are most proud of?" my grandfather responded with, "I don't think you would be surprised if I said that your mother was a bit of a rebel—to the extent that a rare treasure was given to your grandmother and I. You." Reading that as a grown woman, I understood completely that while I may have disappointed my grandfather in the moment with the FUCK incident, on a larger level, in his eyes I was absolutely *fucking* perfect.

11

SOLO
BOOBY

"I would tell mom but everyone thinks I would be too young to have a boyfriend. Boy-friend just means he's a boy and a very good friend. We wouldn't kiss or anything, it just means that I like him more than the other boys in the class and he would like me more than the other girls in the class. I wish I could tell mom."

AMANDA, Grade 5 diary entry

ABOUT A YEAR LATER, my grandma took the position "downtown" to work at the school district's head office as a superintendent, and I was shipped off to Julia Kiniski School to attend class under the tutelage of my aunt Karen. Progressive for its time, the school was organized in multi-grade classrooms; I was placed in a combined grades 4 and 5 class.

One morning sometime around then, I woke up with one boob. After several days of living in horror with this puffy foreigner that looked like it had consumed one too many glasses of white zinfandel the night before, I eventually told my aunt Karen about what was living on my chest. I wanted to know: Was this thing invested in staying for the long haul or just testing out my body to see if I was a viable host?

"What do you mean, *one* boob?" she asked. Then, like I was a circus freak, she shouted, "Let me see it!"

I'm sure she wasn't trying to be insensitive; it's more that she had to see it to believe it. But seriously. "IT." Ugh.

"Um... no way," I said. I was now a woman. I was not going to flash Solo Booby, even if *she* was a bit of a freakshow, like a contortionist with both legs twisted behind her head, awaiting applause from the creeps in the back row.

The conversation stopped abruptly and, like the grown woman I was, I went to sleep in my grandma's room, with a citrus-flavoured nightcap of juice nestled between my arm and Solo Booby.

The next morning, over her butter-laden raisin toast, my aunt said, "You fell asleep last night with your orange juice and soaked Grandma's bed."

What?! I was mortified. I looked down to see the mess only to discover that I was wearing a set of pajamas I had not put on myself. I had no recollection of being changed in the middle of the night. I imagined my limbs flopping about like a milk-drunk baby while Aunt Karen and Solo Booby awkwardly confronted each other. Embarrassed, I poured myself another glass of orange juice, dumped a cinnamon-sugar concoction on my white toast, and retreated to the rumpus room to watch cartoons.

There is simply no other explanation than to think that in my aunt's desperation to see Solo Booby, she had drugged me. Did she have accomplices? Did they all stand around me, laughing and pointing?

My body felt like a hormone-laden petri dish. Not long after that, pubic hair sprouted—something that had *not* been covered in Mrs. S's impromptu sex ed lesson. At my new school, standing on the steps that snaked down to the library, I disclosed to my friend Diana that some kind of extraterrestrial peach fuzz was growing in my nether region. She gave me a casual "Yeah... me too," in a way that revealed her parents had already prepared her for life's inevitable realities. Little did I know then that my own education was just around the corner.

MY PUBESCENT STATE soon had me in heat. I was deep into an estrogen-infused boy mania. This was also the year my fashion sense went from being profoundly my own—obnoxious, vibrant colours, intentionally disharmonious patterns, and a

"Um . . . no way," I said.
I was now a woman.
I was not going to
flash Solo Booby,
even if *she* was a bit
of a freakshow.

mishmash of various styles—to a look curated just to capture the hearts of boys. That is to say, I selected the prettiest and most popular girl in my class—someone who always had little rosy patches under her eyes—and completely ripped off her style. For months, I begged my mom to buy me an official CFL pullover winter jacket with the matching toque and gloves. The day I finally acquired them, I arrived at school with distinct pride as I showed off my crisp, new outdoor gear displaying the Edmonton football team colours of gold and green—only to have that pride dwindle within seconds when the boys, while initially impressed with my *sportiness*, realized that it was still me underneath all that ridiculous sports regalia.

I did eventually have my first foray into the advances of the male species—specifically, of a boy named Kyle. Each afternoon, when we returned from recess, I would find a clear plastic baggie of kid dope in my indoor shoes (and by "dope" I mean junk food). As I rammed my feet into my knock-off Keds, my toes would mash up against the soft, squishy interior of a well-appointed selection of five-cent candies. I give Kyle credit—he certainly knew how to play to his audience. The thing is, I didn't really like him, and that caused a major ethical dilemma: How does one keep their dealer and their "drugs" without ever having to actually pay? In the end, I did tell Kyle I didn't like him *like that*, hoping that he would continue making his daily deliveries anyway. Unsurprisingly, he did not. Hell hath no fury like a dealer scorned.

When it came to my first *real* boyfriend, Robbie, we fell for each other pretty hard. We'd spend each recess walking the perimeter of the schoolyard holding hands, and we played our song—"(Everything I Do) I Do It for You" by Bryan Adams—over and over again on our shared mixtapes. At one point, Robbie used his allowance to buy us matching necklaces, with our first initials on them. I proudly wore his around my neck, and he, mine. Robbie was a nice boy, and his mom was actively involved in the school, constantly volunteering to supervise the students. (She had her eye on us too.)

During a special lunch one day, Robbie consumed eight doughnuts and five cookies and then proceeded to barf all over the place. I got angry with him for being gross and we ended up breaking up shortly afterward. In retrospect, there might have been some adult intervention that led to our first breakup, because when we got back together not long after, we tried to do so without anyone finding out. The secret reconnection didn't last, however—Robbie was proving to be indecisive, and my body, succumbing to full-blown puberty, had no interest in waiting around for him to make up his mind. Quickly, I moved on to a boy named Scott (and if Robbie still liked me, then, as my diary stated at the time, "too bad"). Going by the timeline in my diaries, after Scott came Jeff... then Steve, Randy, David, and Michael.

Thanks to my overbearing grandmother, my escapades with these boys never amounted to anything other than fragmented diary entries that read like I was psychotic. Grandma made it very clear to me, at an early age, that boys were sort of scary and I should watch myself and, most importantly, my reputation, which could be spoiled and never returned to its original condition. So, after the first flush of my adolescent boy mania, that condition was soon replaced by a general fear of the opposite sex and a prudish demeanour that would make Grandma proud.

And as for Solo Booby? Eventually, a brand-new left booby caught up with the early arriving right, though it never quite grew enough to make them both the same size. Come to think of it, my stunted feet also vary in size—my right foot is about half a size larger than my left. What is menopause going to look like? Will just one ovary revolt, forcing me to wait another year for the other one to catch up?

Regarding these medical mysteries of pubescence, if you are a doctor and want to explain them to me, please email me at solobooby@notthatlikeable.com.

12

PEN PALS

"I like art. And going out and having fun on a daily basis. I like Amanda's room because it's always so clean! Amanda is a very special girl, who has a crazy mother."

THE DEB, musing to Amanda in a shared 1990s diary

A **COUPLE YEARS** after I took sex ed with Mrs. S, my mother and I kept a diary together. It was a short-lived exercise—we were pen pals, almost like two strangers under the same roof. Ships passing in the night, forgetting to put our running lights on so that maybe, just maybe, we'd actually see each other instead of leaving a head-on collision to chance. At that time, my mom would have recently turned twenty-nine and was likely busy spending her time crushing Bacardi Breezers and banging her boyfriend, Ron. I'd be at school; she'd be at work. I'd be at my best friend's house; she'd be at a party. I'd be in Banff on a trip with my grandparents; she'd be at the lake with her cronies. The pedestal I had placed her on was so high that it's no wonder it toppled later in my life. As children, we can't fathom that our parents are normal humans with struggles and wants that are separate from our own, even if often only temporary, narcissistic needs.

The diary starts with lists of our goals for that year, written on the inside cover. Well, with one of those lists written out, anyway. Mom never got around to writing hers.

Amanda's 1993 Goals	Mom's 1993 Goals
To get along with mommie	
Stop sleeping in her bed because she probably doesn't like it	

The rest of the diary shows a similarly one-sided commitment:

Dear Mandi,

I hope you realize how much I love you + how precious you are. My life could never be the same without you.

I'm proud to be your mom.

Love, Mom

P.S. I know I'm not exactly your typical mom ("Suzy Home-maker") but maybe one day we'll bake a cake together!!

Dear Mommy,

Can we bake a cake this weekend or sometime? I also love you very much and my life wouldn't be the same without you. You are very special, and I love you a lot. I don't know what I'd do without you. I'm glad you are my mommy. You're the best mommy in the world. Please write back!

Love, Pumpkin

● ● ●

Dear Mommy,

Maybe we can do something on Wednesday because I'm busy Tuesday or we could do it on Friday because I have (and you have) an activity night. Oh! I just heard you're going to Ron's on Wednesday, or was it Tuesday? Or we could do something on Sunday. Oh, and I also heard you're going out with Tony on Sunday, and I have a party to go on Saturday. Write back!

Love your Pest, Amanda

P.S. I love you

* * *

Dear Mommy, I love you.

Please write back because you haven't for a long time! I miss you. ☹ I hope that soon we can go out somewhere, it doesn't have to be anything special. Just to be with you. Have a wonderful week.

Love yours truly, Pumpkin

P.S. DON'T TELL ANYONE THIS. SOMETIMES I CRY AT NIGHT BECAUSE I MISS YOU SO MUCH. EVEN WRITING THIS TO YOU ALMOST MAKES ME CRY. YOU ARE THE ONLY PERSON I CAN TALK TO. You're so special. I guess I just love you too much!

* * *

Dear Mommy,

If anything ever happened to you I'd die.

Love Mandy

For a while, I drop the letter pretext and just write to my mom directly:

I hate grandma. She's mean and never lets me have at least 1 sleepover, AH! I hate her.

Seemingly written three seconds later:

I love her also 'cause she just let me have a sleepover at Diana's house. I love you mommy. Sorry for telling you all my problems but I just needed to let them out.

Grandma's mean. Please buy me and take me to things and places that grandma doesn't approve of. Buy me a bra to make grandma mad. Take me to your friend's house to make her mad. Stand up for me so I don't have to listen to her... Grandma said "to pack my bags and move out" so please get an apartment or something because I'll kill myself if I live here too long. This is misery. I hate this house. Even if grandma forgives me I still want to move out because this happens every day and all I did was show Diana my room and grandma has a hemorrhage!

Love,
The child nobody loves "but you"
P.S. Sorry for telling you my problems

Probably three minutes later:

Me and Grandma are friends again. But to avoid this off-on relationship please move out and take me with you!

Love, Amanda

Then, an actual answer from Mom!

Dear Mandy,

Please don't talk about yourself like that because you're better than that. You should never say hate for it is a strong word of cruelty. Don't say you're going to kill yourself because it's not normal to talk like that. When you feel mad you should think or write down all the good things about yourself + be the positive bright girl you are, remember life can have its ups + downs but there is always happiness. Remember all the people who love you, especially me. My world would never be the same without you. Remember I am going to the lake this weekend. I promise to take you out on Tuesday because Monday I have a class. I love you, precious.

Have a great weekend.

Love you, mom

Later, a couple lines from Mom, again:

Music is a single note written in the writer's quote. The music is unknown until the poet writes the song until whom it may belong.

Dear Mom,

Please don't write poems 'cause I don't understand them. This is supposed to be a book where we talk to each other. The poems are nice but they don't turn me on.

Love,
The Love of Your Life!

Sometime after writing this, I return to continue this note:

My teacher said that we should tell our parents what we learned in sex ed. She said we should feel comfortable about saying things and using correct terms. So here's what we learned. (Please don't show this to anyone.)

When girls get older they grow pubic hair and also with boys. We saw some overheads about a female vagina and a male penis. They showed the reproductive system. I learnt what an orgasm is. For a woman an orgasm is when her vagina gets wet. For a man his penis grows larger and hardens. They showed on a movie how the sperm travels and goes to the egg and the baby forms after a while.

I have one question for you, mom.

What happens during puberty, and how can you tell you are in puberty?

Am I in puberty?

Sincerly, Amanda

P.S. She also said we live with these things every day, we should not be shy to say them.

PLEASE WRITE BACK!!

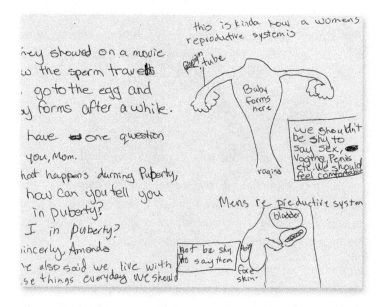

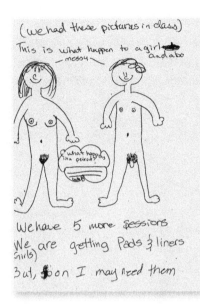

(we had these pictures in class)

This is what happen to a girl → and a bo
~ messy ~

what happens in a period

We have 5 more sessions
We (girls) are getting Pads & liners
But, soon I may need them

Please write ~~Piriod~~ back!

Dear Amanda, you will know when your in pube when you start growing ~~booba~~ breasts, pubic hair & get your piriod. Do me a favour don't be going around talking about orgasms to people. Ex for maybe Addrea be she's your best friend Panty liners are usualy used for a lighter

---

Dear Amanda,

You will know when your in puberty when you start growing boobs [Note: I cross my mother's word out and correct it to "breasts"], *pubic hair + get your piriod* [I skip correcting this one]. *Do me a favour, don't be going around talking about orgasms to people. Except for maybe Andrea because she's your best friend. Panty liners are usually used for a lighter day period* [I give my mom a check mark to inform her that she's spelled period correctly this time] *or just a protectant or just to stay clean and fresh. A piriod* [I correct this to "period"] *comes once a month and lasts about 5 days* [I cross this out and write "2–8 days"]. *You usually have to change your pad according to how heavy your piriod* [I skip this one] *is, and right before bedtime + first thing in the morning. During or before your piriod* [I do catch this one though] *you might get different emotional changes or cramping in your lower abdomen. No you shouldn't be embarrassed to talk about sex, but remember to talk privately to only your good friends, and you don't have to know everything right now because your* [I missed this one] *only 11, anyways things come to mind naturally when you grow older and you learn things in* good *time.*

Love, Mom ☺

Dear Mom,

We had Sex Ed again! (Don't tell anyone this.) My teacher said when you're in puberty a mucous, yolkey stuff comes out. And usually, I have that. So, I am probably going to have my period soon. I think you should pack a kit for me. Please!

Love, Mandie
P.S. I will also take the time of using the kit, using deodorant and taking more showers.

Amanda, I don't need correction on my writeing.

13

NOT THAT
~~LIKEABLE~~

"Don't speak to me in that tone of voice, grandma."

AMANDA, age four, diary entry

"When I'm with gram.ma I know I can be myself."

AMANDA, age five, diary entry

"I hate grandma. She doesn't get me."

AMANDA, age six, diary entry

SEVERAL TIMES A DAY, my grandmother used to sing to me, and I would sing along:

You're the best little girl in the world (yes, you are)
You're the best little girl in the world (yes, you are)
You're sugar and you're spice,
And everything that's nice,
You're grandma's little baby girl.

My grandma was right about one thing: I figuratively and literally *was* sugar. I imagine that a glucose test at that point would have revealed liquid sugar running through my veins. I was also spice—and as I reflect on this, I wonder if this single song was the catalyst for that dichotomy in my personality. One minute I'm welling up in tears over a dog meme and the next, I'm screaming in my car at the person who is driving the exact speed limit in front of me (because *everyone* knows that you can go ten kilometres over).

My grandmother had returned from her stint as super-intendent and was transferred to St. Teresa—and, since she was my ride, I switched schools again. Grade 6 signalled the beginning of a great many things. First, I adopted the habit of wearing a black, ribbed, long-sleeved, cotton mock-neck shirt under everything I wore. It didn't matter if it was a cropped tank, a Guess T-shirt, or a crocheted vest, I rocked this mock-neck under everything. My plucky boobs were starting to grow in, and, without a training bra, it was a perfect way to mask my pint-size torpedo tits.

This is also the year that, despite my complaints, my parents did not believe that I needed glasses. In their defence, I had repeatedly asked for glasses (and braces) several times in the past just because I thought they were *super cool*. While we could pontificate on where I obtained my frame of reference for what was "cool," I think we can all agree that I was very likely misled. While the other girls were smothering themselves in CK One and leaning into velvet chokers and choppy Jennifer Aniston–inspired lobs, I was itching to add layers of metal and glass to my face. It wasn't until my teacher Mr. M noticed me squinting at the board that I was sent back to the optometrist for a recheck.

Mock-neck making a summertime appearance.

It didn't matter if it was a cropped tank, a Guess T-shirt, or a crocheted vest, I rocked this mock-neck under everything.

I came home from that visit with round John Lennon-esque tortoiseshell frames that gave me a very studious vibe, which was something I could really get behind. Given my last experience under my grandmother's watch, I was doing everything I could to stay out of trouble. I was no longer the little girl who wrote profanities on the blackboard. Instead, my new friend group consisted of my homeroom teacher and the school librarian, Mrs. A. Instead of playing Pokémon after school, I was charging up the dinosaur "tablets" that pre-dated today's iPads on the classroom cart.

One of the things I loved most about being a teacher's pet was that I was often called upon to help set up the bulletin board. I fondly recall weekend trips to the "teacher store" with my grandmother, where I would help pick from the many colours of corrugated papers and pair them with the seasonal or topical scalloped borders to line the boards with. I always took great care crafting these feature walls, as the ridges of the paper would easily dent if not handled properly. Little did I know that my deep respect for corrugated paper would lead to social suicide.

Like most kids in school, my classmates had been together since kindergarten. As I jumped from school to school, I was always the exception to this rule, and at St. Teresa, I was, at best, a curious outsider coming in and disrupting a harmonious ecosystem with my black mock-neck shirt and puffy nips.

At lunch, we would line up to attempt the perfect nuke on our Pizza Pops before they burst. We each had our individual techniques: some kids heated theirs in a plastic container with the lid loosely resting on top, others would put them on a plate and disregard the crunchy crust this technique caused. My method was to wrap my Pizza Pop in a paper towel and place it directly on the rotating dish. The success rate was about 50/50, and triumph usually involved sustaining second-degree burns on the roof of my mouth from the scalding cheesy core. (Failure was having the gooey interiors spilling out in a waste on the glass plate in the microwave. No, I never cleaned it up.)

Over one of these lunch hours, I happened upon one of the popular boys, Seth, who was loitering in the classroom. I wanted to fit in, so I joined him.

"Whad'ya doin'?" I asked. I was unsuccessfully attempting to shovel my Pizza Pop into my mouth without dropping the contents of it all over my black mock-neck.

"Nothin'," he said. He ran the tip of his nail horizontally across the vertical ridges of the corrugated paper edging the corkboard.

Ugh… What is he doing? Doesn't he know how expensive that paper is?

"Um, like, careful. That paper, uh, marks super easy," I said casually, using my cheese-laden paper towel to remove the remaining crust crumbs from my chin.

"You should write something," he said, ignoring my warning.

A wave of shame and nausea rushed over me as I recalled trying to convince Maryanne to write "FUCK" on the blackboard.

"Nah," I said. *No fucking way am I getting set up for round two of a suspension from my grandmother.*

As if reading my mind, Seth started to etch "FUCK" into the corrugated paper, looking over his shoulder, daring me to make him stop.

But now, in my new role as a goody two-shoes, it only seemed appropriate that I make up for the bad karma I had inflicted earlier. As soon as Seth finished, I nonchalantly walked out of the room, and then tore away as quickly as I could to go tell on him.

Then, shit went sideways.

"Why did you have to tell me about that, Amanda? Why did you have to tattle on that boy?" my grandmother demanded.

"Because... because he wrote a bad word!" I stammered.

"You know what I have to do now? I have to suspend the boy. Do you know who Seth's dad is?"

"Um... no. But... Grandma, he wrote a bad word on the board!"

"Seth is Mr. T's son—Mr. T, my vice principal!"

I was dumbfounded. Here I was, literally trying to uphold the sacred walls of teachers everywhere—and I was being punished for it.

Shortly after this unfortunate situation, I noticed a massive change in the student body towards my general existence. I was no longer welcomed, included, or acknowledged by the boys or girls in either of the Grade 6 classes. I became an outlier. Recess was lonely; I was nameless other than by my new title of "Tattletale." I fell into a serious funk—a depression, really—that lasted for months and resulted in my grandmother lightly chastising me for my dejected demeanour.

"Do you want to be a ray of sunshine or a gloomy rain cloud?" she would ask during our long drives to and from school each day. I would shrug and tell her what she wanted to hear: that I wanted to be a ray of sunshine, of course. I just wanted to make her proud of me. *I wanted to be liked.*

Those pep talks didn't help. Eventually, my grandmother decided that my funk had gone too far, and, with good intentions, she decided to conspire on a solution with both of the Grade 6 teachers at the school. I had morphed into a social pariah, and they were committed to fixing the situation. What happened next was the most mortifying moment of my entire existence.

Over one of the lunch hours, I was minding my own business, moonlighting as Edmonton Catholic School's youngest

IT department member and doing a little tune-up on the school's tech. My grandmother came by and asked me to come with her to the art room. Given my history of assisting with colourful overhead projector transparencies, I assumed that some new creative project was about to be dumped in my lap, and I was happy to oblige. As I stepped into the art room, I was met with the faces of every single Grade 6 girl from both classes. There were thirty sets of eyes on me, likely filled with a pity soup of disgust, indifference, and pubescent angst.

I stopped short at the entrance, but my grandmother gently pushed me over to one of the chairs near the front of the room. One of the teachers launched into a dissertation on the effects of bullying and how the unkind behaviour everyone was showing was affecting me. Basically, these girls were all told they couldn't tease me anymore, and they *had* to be my friends.

Amanda, *actually* wearing panties, and Grandma.

I was not prone to blushing, but at that moment my cheeks burned crimson. Pity hung like smoke in the darkest corner of a casino. My future popularity was in the hands of the student body—and the house, well, it always wins.

Over the weeks that followed, one of the girls did soften her disdain for me and reached out to "be friends." I suspect it was because her mother and my grandmother were in cahoots, but nonetheless, Catherine, her younger sister, and I became rather close, and I ended up spending quite a bit of time at her house. We were really into fabric paint, and I covered almost everything I owned in brightly coloured goo— pillowcases, jean shorts, T-shirts. The problem is, I never trusted it—I never trusted that someone could like me enough to be my friend. Still, I masked that disbelief with resolute confidence, held up by a deep need to be loved.

I know my grandmother meant well and I don't fault her—she was the OG Helicopter Parent. In her eyes, I *was* deserving of great love (no, but seriously, that's what "Amanda" actually means). But despite or perhaps because of her efforts, I developed distrust in the friendships I had at that school, always feeling sure that the girls would eventually let me down—even after some had developed into steadfast friends. It didn't really matter, though. I never stuck around long enough to find out.

14

THE
DARK
YEARS

"I went to bed that night both anxious and excited about school the next day. Nightmares about junior high flooded my head."

AMANDA, Grade 7 book report

AFTER WHAT WAS a rather tumultuous termination of elementary school for me, my family of educators (aka The FOE) determined that having me follow my Grade 6 classmates to the same junior high was out of the question—after all, that same FOE had basically reverse-bullied those kids into being my friends.

So, the summer leading up to Grade 7 was fuelled by trepidation and veiled zest. As a seasoned brown-noser, I had so far been protected by my familial connections within the school system, but now I was about to step out from under that wing, and I couldn't have been more ill prepared for the onslaught of pain—however partially self-inflicted—that was about to come my way. If the school supply list had included "duct tape for mouth," it would have saved me a lot of heartache.

Somewhere around this time, I developed an overwhelming obsession with the notion of having "cool" panties. This might sound a touch unlikely given the rather cavalier attitude I had taken towards displaying my vulva when I was in daycare, but I was and still am a pro-underwear kind of gal. Before this obsession set in, I was likely wearing what all pre-teen girls wore at that time: tighty-whities with some sort of floral print that basically acted as a modern-day chastity belt. What I *really, really* wanted was a teal, fuchsia, and purple tri-pack of high-waisted, full-back Hanes Her Way. Looking back, I wonder if Hanes had rereleased their overstock from the late '80s to the unsuspecting teenagers who were forced to buy their undergarments from the local discount department store, SAAN (2008, RIP).

My preoccupation with these vibrant panties was so extraordinary that I went so far as to write and illustrate a short piece of fiction that chronicled a blossoming young woman entering a rather sensitive time in her life—junior high. I certainly was not being subtle when I presented this "fable" to my grandparents in an attempt to inspire them to buy them for me. I suspect it was my grandfather who was finally tasked with taking me to SAAN to procure the "cool" panties. (In a perfect world, this might also have been an appropriate time to purchase a training bra for me.)

Cool, grown-up panties in place, I was enrolled in Grade 7 at Victoria Composite, a school for the arts. For the first time, they had extended their programming to allow for junior high student enrollment, and The FOE thought this would be a great solution to my free-spirited approach to education. "Free-spirited" meaning I could do whatever the fuck I wanted as long as I was "being good."

Although you present excellent writing skills and a great sense of enthusiasm, you need to review the CRITERIA of the assignments.

—Grade 7 language arts teacher's response to my report on Anne Frank

This school had no business allowing me access to its artsy, inner-city halls filled with graceful dancers, natural musicians, fine artists, and dramatic performers. While I may have been Best in Show at other schools, what talent I had, while innate, was scrappy and untrained. I went from being a big fish in a little pond to just a regular fish in a weird pond. It was my first time experiencing imposter syndrome: I didn't feel good enough to be at this school.

In preparation for each school year, my grandma would take me shopping. It was both a tradition for us to share and a necessary step to ensure that my appearance didn't reflect poorly on the Whelan name. For Grade 7, Grandma didn't disappoint. We made a very special trip to Le Château to pick out an appropriate "first day outfit."

To think that Britney Spears was the first person to normalize the naughty schoolgirl vibe would be to overlook *my* debut, which occurred four years prior to the release of "... Baby One More Time." On the first day of school, which was also the day of our school photos, I proudly donned what I felt was one of the hippest ensembles that would ever grace the pages of the Victoria Composite yearbook: a crisp, white, long-sleeved button-down shirt, a black crocheted vest, white knee-high socks, patent leather Mary Janes, and a red and black pleated plaid skirt. My hair was pulled back in a bun, secured with a matching plaid scrunchie, and I was still sporting my round-rimmed glasses. Put together, this look transported me into the first five minutes of some bad amateur pornography production—one that would have inevitably ended with me naked on a desk being taught a lesson by "Teacher." Didn't The FOE know better than to send me into an inner-city school dressed like an amateur porn star?

A few weeks into the school year, I ended up home sick for several days. I couldn't explain how I was feeling: just sore and tired, with a dull ache that pervaded my groin area. After three days on the sofa, I rose in the morning feeling like a new woman. I headed to the washroom for a pee and to contemplate what stylish get-up I would sport on my return

"Are you from a private school?" —Toby

to school. Looking down at the wad of toilet paper (doesn't everyone do this?), I saw a smear of blood against the white paper. And. I. Totally. Freaked. Out.

"Oh my God, oh my God, oh my God," I said, tossing the TP into the toilet with repulsion. I pulled up my pajama pants so quickly that the waist ended up resting underneath Solo Booby and its smaller sidekick, Robin. I let out a moan of confusion and burst into my mom's bedroom.

I shook her to wake her up.

"Mom, Mom... Mom!!"

She rolled over, smelling like Fast Eddies. She had a few days off work and had opted to let loose at her favourite neighbourhood joint.

"Whad'ya want?" she grumbled.

"Mom! I'm bleeding! I THINK I'M DYING!"

She propped herself up in bed and looked me up and down, trying to ascertain where exactly the bleeding was coming from.

"What the hell are you talking about?" she said, lying back down.

"When I went to the bathroom... there was, there was..." I lowered my voice. "Blood..."

"Oh, pumpkin, you just got your period."

I immediately started crying. "I'm scared, Mom."

But I wasn't scared. I was shocked. Since the days when I had shared a diary with my mom, I had never learned anything else in school about puberty, and, quite frankly, I had forgotten most of what I had been taught. Mom never did get me a "kit," so I can be grateful, at least, that this entrance into womanhood took place at home and not in gym class.

"Go into your grandmother's bedroom and get a maxi-pad out of her drawer."

My grandmother was at school already, so I rummaged around her room and procured myself a pad.

I went back into my mom's room. "Got it. Now what?" I asked.

"Go put it in your underwear, you nut!" She gave me a gentle squeeze and rolled over.

As I unwrapped the pad from its peach-coloured plastic, it appeared much larger and bulkier than I had expected. How was this miniature diaper supposed to fit in my underwear? The extra-long, super-thick overnight pad was seriously dumpy.

Instead of being able to select a cute outfit that accentuated my slim frame, I returned to school sporting my clunky diaper and whatever clothing would hide it as it swished around like a candy wrapper in my pants. I'm sure my entire under-carriage had an abrasion wound by the time I returned home.

Even though we were taught that our period would come once a month and generally with some warning, I felt that somehow I would be different and it would try to fuck me over. So, every day for the rest of Grade 7, I wore a dou-ble layer of protection: one super absorptive pad stuck atop a panty liner, just in case. Given this lack of knowledge, I also told my gym teacher that I could no longer partake in swimming during gym—my favourite activity—because I was afraid that the moment I dipped into the cool chlorine, a crime scene would explode from my body. Instead, I spent the gym hour hanging out with the silverfish that procreated at record speed within the dingy locker room.

Later on that year, I managed to secure one real friend, Kerianne. We were both total dorks with our Coke bottle glasses, questionable sense of style, and bizarre, dry sense of humour that most people didn't get. I knew Kerianne was a *real* friend (and not being paid by my grandma) when she told me I needed a bra. She and I would often disappear together over lunch to find some deserted, bully-free area of the school and basically dick around for forty-five minutes,

For the rest of Grade 7, I wore a double layer of protection: one super absorptive pad stuck atop a panty liner, just in case.

doing our best to avoid any humans who might take offence to our general appearance. One day, when I went to school wearing a thin, white ribbed top that laced up the front, we were doing just that when Kerianne pointed at my boobs and asked, "Don't you have a bra?"

"I don't need to wear a bra," I said. I truly did believe this. Both boobs had finally started to grow in (albeit not evenly), but I still just had two swollen lumps atop my bony frame. What would a bra do?

Kerianne looked at me with disbelief. She had a crooked smile with equally crooked teeth, and soft, kind eyes. "Umm… yes, you do," she said.

I looked down at my relatively flat chest, trying to make sense of her comment. There could have been, at best, small inflections on either side of my chest that warranted a bra.

"Are you sure? Like, I'm so flat."

"Not as flat as me and I'm wearing a bra." She dipped the shoulder of her shirt down and exposed a delicate lace strap.

I can't remember exactly who I told when I got home, but that evening my aunt Karen made my grandfather drive me back to SAAN to buy a training bra. To be fair, you can hardly call what we bought a bra, as it was basically just a couple of flaps of lace sewn together that offered no actual support. But by spurring me to enclose my adolescent boobs in those thin bits of cloth, Kerianne had made her best attempt at leading me towards social acceptability.

Unfortunately, just as you can't make the proverbial horse drink the proverbial water, it turned out that you can't make a preteen Amanda look after her own best social interests. So, since my Grade 7 self was clearly hell-bent on collecting cautionary lessons, I will present them here to you now so that any young people who may be reading this book can at least learn a thing or two from them. Grab your highlighter and be prepared to take notes (maybe even a pen for reflections in the margin if you are reading this in print), because here comes my own proprietary three-step guide to making sure you never fit in or earn the respect of your peers at any point in your junior high school experience, ever. Starting with...

STEP ONE: LAUNCH A PURITAN MOVEMENT

Each morning of Grade 7, I would enter through the south doors, which led to the main hall that housed all the home-rooms for the junior high students. That's where the smokers hung out, so I would always have to walk through billows of noxious smoke that, in my opinion, was often intentionally being blown in my face.

One might assume that I had a greater tolerance of second-hand smoke given my mother's lifelong addiction, but in my effort to "be good," I had never smoked myself. So, about four weeks into the school year, I started an anti-smoking campaign. Yes, you heard me correctly. In Grade 7, at the bottom of the coolness food chain, I launched a full-scale anti-smoking movement by circulating a petition to ban smoking on all school property. While I hadn't yet discovered Excel or my love for sophisticated formulas, I drew my own grid by hand to capture the names of the many students who would obviously be lining up to sign my petition. I went at it for weeks, trolling the halls between classes for others who would join my cause. Apart from five or six brave students who perhaps were only taking pity on me and had no idea what they were agreeing to, no one would put their name on the sheet.

Even if I was embarrassed by the extreme brevity of my petition, I still handed it in to my homeroom teacher, made

About four weeks into the school year, I started an anti-smoking campaign. Yes, you heard me correctly.

my case, and, inevitably, admitted defeat when I saw the pity that she too wore on her face. After that, I started to enter the school from a different set of doors so I could avoid the smoke (and my growing disregard for the inevitable COPD victims who wouldn't succumb to my concern for their health). Those who had previously tolerated me in home-room now gave me the side-eye as I entered class to find a seat. No one would speak to me for fear of being aligned with my priggish manner. It was just me and my unsullied lungs against the world.

STEP TWO: DRESS LIKE AN ASSHOLE

Still oblivious to the fact that I was once again recasting myself in the role of persona non grata, I threw myself into planning for the upcoming Earth Day as an opportunity to express—verbally and visually—my commitment to a healthy planet. I had already developed a strong predilection for wav-ing the green flag, like the time I scolded my grandma for littering out the window of her Celica by asking, "Grandma, are you a friend of the environment?"

About a week out from this internationally celebrated date and just a few days after entering my teens, I was already plan-ning how best to make a statement of support for that very environment. I determined that the most effective display would be an impactful "costume" to honour Mother Earth. When most girls were focused on finding the best CoverGirl powder shade (hint: "Ghost White") or searching the aisles for the Clearasil acne wash, I was busy trivializing Earth Day by turning it into a solo costume party.

Picture this: It is Thursday, April 20, 1995. My thirteenth birthday. My grandpa and my two uncles are half-watching

Star Trek: Voyager as they lament over the end of *Star Trek: The Next Generation*. In the background, my grandma is working at her desk—as she does every evening—and revealing her closet-romantic nature by calling out that they should put on *Mad About You* instead. As for me, I *should* be out celebrating the official onset of my teens by dabbling in drugs or stealing shit with my friends. But instead, as Earth Day is on Saturday and I have planned to honour the event at school on the Friday before, I'm spending my birthday making a trash-bag smock to wear to school the next day. This noble work includes rummaging under the sink for an oversized black garbage bag, cutting a large hole for my head and two holes for my arms into said bag, digging through the neighbour's trash for stuff that was tossed instead of being put in the recycling bin so I can use it as a shame display, and, finally, stapling those wasted recyclables onto my makeshift poncho for the final effect.

I think you can imagine the response from the crew of Grade 7s at school the next day, which included a mad dash away from my general vicinity. You know that moment when you are watching a particularly bad movie and the foreshadowing is so glaringly palpable or obvious that you can hardly watch out of embarrassment for the character? That basically sums up that entire Friday.

STEP THREE: RUIN POTENTIAL FRIENDSHIPS

My school held an annual fundraising auction where people could bid on other students to help them out with small tasks for a day. I had bid on my quasi-friend Jason. I say "quasi-friend" because while we had met at the Fringe festival the summer before and shared a love of choir and music, he was still a bit wary of my antics. Over time, though, I think he came to grow a bit fond of me, despite my terrible reputation, strange escapades, and questionable fashion sense. What I wanted Jason to do was help me clean out my locker, which was a complete dumpster fire.

Because my family had never put any kind of expectation on me to keep my room or belongings orderly, there was no exception when it came to my locker. Among all the reams of unsorted paper, Duo-Tang'ed book reports, and stale gym clothes, stacks of uneaten lunches had piled up and were busily decomposing. As Jason dug into this hoarder's paradise to start sorting out my filth, a rotten apple rolled out of the locker and into the middle of the hallway.

"Oh my God. No." Jason jumped away from the science experiment that was formerly my locker. "This is so gross—no."

I wasn't embarrassed because I didn't know any better.

"Um... I paid good money for this. It's for charity. You gotta do it," I said. I stood next to him like a tyrant in front of her people, holding open my locker door as he glared at me. Like a champ, he continued to pull at the contents of my scholastic detritus until I was satisfied. Later in the year, I developed a bit of a crush on Jason and when I expressed this boldly to his friends, I was met with disdain. *You and Jason? No fucking way.*

ALL OF THESE poorly executed strategies did earn me some pretty predictable results—though, as I am ever grateful for, I did have one steadfast defender. On the last day of school, long after my locker had returned to its natural state of revolting pigsty, we were expected to fully clear out our belongings for the summer months. I realized that I had far underestimated how much stuff I was going to have to take home, and my backpack was fully maxed out. I couldn't bear to part with my Earth Day trash smock, all those liquid-soaked class papers, and the soiled bags from many months of lunches, and decided that, since it was only a single bus ride home, I could manage to carry it all.

I knew my irregularly overactive bladder wouldn't last until I got home, so, with a heavy load upon my back and my arms stacked high with the most valuable trash pile you've ever seen, I made my way to the girl's washroom. As I was struggling with my things and trying to open the door to the washroom, a Grade 9 girl I'll call "Hall Demon" approached.

"Hey, Amanda! Can I help you with those?" she said.

This girl had often been rather unkind to me over the course of the year, but this time it seemed like perhaps she was bent on making amends—after all, school was out for the summer! Maybe she realized it wasn't too late for her to turn over a new leaf, atone for her missteps, and decide to start the next year with me as super best friends. I'd be in Grade 8, she'd be in Grade 10—this was going to catapult me into popularity.

"Um... yeah. That would be, like, so great. Thank you so much! I just have to pee!"

I passed all my treasures out of my arms and into hers and walked into the washroom. I saw that Kerianne was already in there, and we grabbed stalls next to each other.

"Oh my gosh! I, like, have so much stuff!" I called over the partition. "Hall Demon from Grade 9 is totally helping me and is holding all my stuff outside the door. Isn't that, like, so nice?"

"Um, doesn't she hate you?" Kerianne inquired.

"No, we are, like, totally cool now. She totally asked to help me out!"

I left the stalls first, and as I washed my hands, I yelled, "I'll meet you in the hall!" over the noise of the taps. Then I went out to collect my things from my new friend.

I couldn't bear to part with my Earth Day trash smock, all those liquid-soaked class papers, and the soiled bags from many months of lunches.

To my surprise, as I pulled the door open, there was a large trash can right in front of the doorway. It was partially filled with the discarded locker remains of students who didn't have the same level of sentiment I carried.

I looked up, confused. *Weird... what is this doing here?*

Then I saw that all of my stuff had been dumped in the middle of the hall. Hall Demon was standing next to the pile. She gestured to the garbage can. "Get in."

"Sorry, what?" *She must be joking*, I thought.

"Get in the garbage can, you fucking idiot."

I froze.

Just then, Kerianne came out of the washroom. Her eyes narrowing behind her greasy lenses, she said, "She's not getting into that."

I turned to look at Kerianne, marvelling at her ability to stand up to this bully.

"Come on, Amanda, let's go," she said, confidently pushing the trash can aside to clear a path for us.

"I'll get you next year!" Hall Demon called out.

As I gathered up my pile of locker goodies from the floor, a small rubber ball dispensed itself from the mass of junk and danced down the hall. And much like that, I too bounced off—to yet another school.

15

MO' SCHOOLS, MO' PROBLEMS

BFF

"Amanda, please don't be a poo head."

ANDREA, Grade 8, annoyed with my constant girl drama

FELT LIKE I was constantly on the run from being the biggest loser, but I still kept ending up in the same position, as each new school's least lovable newbie. Over and over, I tried to fit in. But my holier-than-thou attitude towards "cool" teen behaviours like mid-class acid dropping and smoking in the ravine was not helping my case.

First and foremost, I realized that Andrea—remember my bestest friend in the whole world?—had been gratuitously embellishing her popularity at St. Kevin's, where I was now joining her for Grade 8. Other than way back in Grade 1, we had never attended school together; our friendship had been preserved by the proximity of our houses and the alleyway between them. When I arrived at this new school, I was expecting to be graciously accepted into the cool friend group she was constantly talking about, and then to immediately rise to the top of school stardom. This was simply what was going to happen. Every time I mentioned her name, I expected people to gush over my rad "older sister," but I was instead repeatedly met with a "Sorry, who?" I suspect that Andrea, like many teenagers, meant well by her talk and was trying to find her place just like I was. And while it turned out that I wasn't going to be able to ride her coattails into popularity, she did keep my secret about being a super loser, including the attempted garbage can shaming that ended my time at my last school.

All in all, the year started off okay. The group of girls who absorbed me into their pack had managed to find a niche in the blurred lines between popularity and complete obscurity. This is when I met my next bestest friend in the world, Amanda Nordstrom, the aforementioned girl with the high pants. Sharing the same first name, among many other similarities, made us fast friends—I could write a whole book about our antics together, but I honestly wouldn't even know where to start. There was the time we wore complete sets of rain gear in her parents' hot tub, or the time when we filmed sexy videos in our bras to Ace of Base, or the time we were trolling 97th Street so we could see what a peep show looked like—but frankly, we were busy having way too much fun together for me to write in my diaries about her. Looking back over the notes we passed in class and the soliloquies we drafted while we were away from each other during summer break makes me appreciate our friendship even more today. She has always been my number one fan, even during times when I was so wrapped up in my own bullshit that I couldn't see how much she needed my friendship in return.

But in terms of our social lives back then, suffice to say that Bestie Amanda was known as "the girl who wears her pants too high," which to this day she defends as a requirement of "having a long torso." (A story that doesn't jibe because a short torso would make your pants look high. Sorry, Amanda, the jig is up and revealed here for all the world to see.) Also in this pack were Stephanie (the bubbly girl-next-door kinda chick), Eme (who had cool parents that would let us stay up until 4 a.m. playing video games), and Kristen (who always had a stash of Fudgee-Os in the crawl space under her basement). Kristen and Stephanie had met playing soccer

Bestie Amanda was known as "the girl who wears her pants too high," which to this day she defends as a requirement of "having a long torso."

Amanda and Amanda: Clearly over bangs.

in Grade 5 and were super tight, and Eme and Amanda had been friends since Grade 1. We all joined as a group in junior high. It was at about this time that my friendship with Andrea began to dissolve quite a bit, and to this day I still feel a little bad about that. Sometimes I feel like I sacrificed that friendship to save myself and find my pack. (Luckily, we still stay in touch today and laugh often about our scissoring Barbies.)

But overall, for the first time in a long time, things felt like they were actually going okay. I had what I thought were real friends who seemed genuinely interested in my companionship (and who, once again, weren't being paid by Grandma—at least, I don't think so). My grandparents were likely happy to see me with real friends and to host this gaggle of girls who left nail polish residue and crumbs in the wake of non-stop sleepovers in their living room. When we weren't monopolizing my grandparents' house, we could usually be found in Kristen's basement, video recording our rendition of *Joseph and the Amazing Technicolour Dreamcoat* or concocting new lyrics in an a cappella group we called Bum Thugs n' Harmony. Here's one that really hit:

Bum, bum, bum, bum, bum, bum, bum.
Tell me whatcha gonna do,
you're stinking up the room,
wear some perfume,
meet me at the outhouse, outhouse, outhouse,
meet me at the outhouse, outhouse, outhouse.

But then, things suddenly got bad. Really, really bad. Around this time, my grandparents got me my own phone line. It was rather out of character for them, as my grandpa did not indulge in unnecessary expenses. I wasn't allowed to play video games or watch most television shows, but my grandparents were content to let me sit and talk on the phone for hours and hours on end. I don't even remember asking for it—it just showed up one day. I think my grandma wanted to have the house phone line back so she could return to gossiping with her school friends. (As I write this, my grandparents are the only people I know who a) have a landline, b) have a landline that has never, ever had an answering machine, and c) have been locked into the same telephone contract since the dawn of time and therefore have the absolute cheapest phone bill I've ever seen.)

One evening, Stephanie and I were chatting on the phone, probably nattering on about boys and what was going on in school. Stephanie's older sister, Emily, was in Grade 9 and was hanging around with the "cool" girls, who spent a lot of time smoking and skipping class. This was when the "Seattle grunge" vibe was going strong, and I'm quite sure Value Village saw a massive uptick in its sales mix for plaid shirts, vintage tees, and cords.

"She looks like a druggie," I said about one of the Grade 9 girls. To be fair, I hardly knew her, but from my limited knowledge of what a druggie looked like—dyed black hair, heavy black eyeliner, and layers of indiscriminate black clothing— she fit the bill. In hindsight, maybe she was just goth. Either way, she fucking terrified my straitlaced bones.

"Yeah, totally. Right?!" Stephanie said, egging me on.

"She totally does drugs," I continued, affirming my position as an expert on those who used drugs. (You know, from watching all the heavy Christian programming like *7th Heaven* on The CW. Life lessons, let me tell you.)

"Yeah, she totally does drugs. So gross, right?" Stephanie said.

We hung up shortly thereafter from what I considered to be a pretty harmless conversation—one that, to be fair, might have been close to accurate. If there was any doubt among the student body that this girl did drugs, she erased it by dressing like she was from a satanic coven… plus, there had been rumours that she had once brought a dead cat in a grocery bag to her classes (rumours that, to be honest, were probably the same kind of mean-spirited crap being thrown my way). What I didn't know was that Emily was listening in on the line and was also friends with said druggie girl.

When I arrived at school the next day… Shit. Hit. The. Fan. Several of the Grade 9 girls (whose names have been scratched out of my yearbook or I'd name them here), who had previously never given me the time of day, started calling me "Prep." Apparently, during this short-lived grunge phase, being judgy *and* wearing Aldo boots, flared jeans, baby tees, and pink eyeshadow made me not only a "prep" but also a total social pariah. Three girls in particular, none of them otherwise memorable, started making my days at school a living hell—tormenting me, threatening me, calling me names, and cornering me at my locker (which thankfully by this time had more photos of JTT than it did rotten lunches).

One of the girls in my class, Amber, hung around with the older girls but also had friends from our own grade. She had long, dark hair that was split into a million little braids, and I used to watch them sway back and forth as she outran me in the 100-metre sprint (she was the only person who could). She also had a bit of a temper. I remember her constantly fighting with Philip, a nerdy but insanely smart boy in our class. They hated each other, and, on one occasion, I think one of them threw a garbage can at the other (or maybe it was a desk?). I like to think they were having a secret love affair they couldn't come to terms with.

"Want to go for a walk at lunch?" Amber asked me one day.

While I was surprised by the invitation, I was still blind to what she was doing. Yes, we were only acquaintances, but she had generally been nice to me, and I thought she was super cool—she had "bad bitch" energy I wanted to hone for myself, so I was happy for the chance to get to know her.

The lunch bell rang and I met Amber at her locker. The halls were unusually quiet, and we chatted for a bit before we left the school to walk over to a field that was a few blocks from the school.

Amber seemed genuinely interested in my life and asked a lot of questions about my family and friends, even telling me a few stories about herself. I was thinking, *We are going to be great friends!*

When we were almost at the field, the grunge pack arrived. I was scared—we were off school grounds and there were no teachers to come to my rescue. I had abandoned my friends to go for a walk with someone I hardly knew. But Amber just kept talking, which made me feel safe—if only for a short moment, because soon the grunge pack moved in and circled around us. I was expecting Amber to tell them to beat it, but instead, she turned and joined them in calling me "Prep" and shouting expletives at me. Suddenly, I realized that the entire Grade 9 student body had come over and was crowding around us in the field. Some kids from Grade 8 were there, too, likely drawn by the crowd and wanting to see who was about to get their ass whupped.

It took absolutely every ounce of my being to calmly turn myself around and walk back to the school, where surely a teacher would take pity on me and pull me into their classroom for protection against this band of bullies. Amber and the grunge pack followed me all the way back to school, screaming at me and telling me they were going to kick my ass. Despite their threats, it never happened. I arrived safely back at school—without shitting myself in terror—and then hid in the bathroom until the bell rang for class to start.

Amber and the grunge pack followed me all the way back to school, screaming at me and telling me they were going to kick my ass.

It took weeks, maybe months, for the consequences of my druggie comment to subside. And to this day, I have never done drugs. For a long time, I wore this fact as a badge of honour because it was never easy. I was constantly pressured, teased, and judged for abstaining. There is this idea that going to a good Catholic school can help kids avoid the issues they'd face at the "public" schools, but I think we just did a better job of hiding it. Throughout junior high and high school, I saw rampant use of drugs among my fellow students. I recall a particularly traumatizing moment when two girls I knew were tripping out in the bathroom during third period—Mr. C's shop class. There I was, taking a pee break from sanding my CO_2 car into the perfect aerodynamic shape, only to stumble upon one of those girls curled up under the vanity, clasping at her hair and having a psychotic break. It was like one of the movies that Grandma, with her dystopian view of the world, wouldn't let me watch, and yet there I was experiencing it in the real world—and I was *wide*-eyed. If the bullying I had faced from the grunge pack hadn't solidified my distaste for the drug life, then that shocking scene certainly did. Straight-edge Amanda 4 lyfe.

16

ON GIRLS /
ON BOYS

"I just farted.
Katya and I are still in a fight."

AMANDA, age thirteen, filled with angst

NO ONE HATES OR LOVES like a thirteen-year-old girl. They hate their enemies, they sometimes hate their friends, and—way too often and way too deeply—they can really hate themselves. Thirteen is also that age when, for girls especially, everything and everyone around you is flipping and turning and flipping again: friends, loyalties, crushes, sense of self. For me, Grade 8 was such a blur that I can hardly remember it: after-school soccer practice, basketball tournaments, endless sleepovers, countless hours at the mall—and so much churn and turmoil in my friendship and dating life that I could hardly keep the names straight, even then. All I know is that the relationships I had coming out of that year were much different than they were going in. Luckily, I have my diaries, which tell a clearer (if chaotic) story than I could ever reconstruct from memory.

So, I'm going to let those pages tell the story of Grade 8 on my behalf (with a brief pause to introduce you to the cast of characters who defined this crazy, fraught, self-flagellating year). Prepare for lots of drama, lots of fighting, lots (lots!) of painful self-deprecation, and just a little bit of shared gum.

THE CAST OF GRADE 8

Janessa (aka Jan): Star soccer player who always got the boys. I sometimes got her sloppy seconds.

Katya: Sophisticated and mature. With her natural Polish beauty, she taught me how to pluck my eyebrows (maybe a bit too much) and properly round brush my hair.

Andrea: This one, you know. My beloved first bestest, always in my heart.

Stephen: Star soccer player. I crushed hard on him for, like, seven seconds, but he never liked me back. Later, I dated his older brother, which was *way* cooler.

Eric: Some random dude.

Kelsey: Another star soccer player... well, actually, *the* star player. Apparently, I had a thing for sporty people. She was too cool to be my friend but, I think, took pity on me.

Matt: Random online dude.

Jamie: Another random online dude.

Amanda Z: Yet another Amanda, just to confuse you. AZ and Kelsey were close friends and both part of the Ukrainian program at our school. They both were really nice to me, and the fact that they lived in two-storey houses (can you imagine?) and had cute clothes they let me borrow made me feel like there might be hope for me after all.

Marc: My first love.

Leon: Boy I crushed on for a really long time despite him always looking like he had just rolled out of bed.

No one hates or loves like a thirteen-year-old girl.

Elizabeth: A very smart, preppy girl in the Ukrainian program who had the absolute best smile.

T.J.: Random pen pal dude.

Petro: Short dude who is probably tall and jacked now.

Marko: A dude who liked Andrea, but he and another dude got into a fight over her, so she refused to date either of them.

Amanda: Me, your faithful narrator and diarist, purging my soul on these inked pages with you, dear reader. Try not to cringe too loudly.

● ● ●

December 22, 1995
Janessa and Stephen were Frenching again—God! That's gross, they do it all the time and I haven't even had a peck on the cheek, let alone a kiss on the lips or a French. *[Um... what did I think the difference was between a French kiss and the "gross" Frenching that Janessa and Stephen were doing?]* Usually when I find out my crush doesn't like me, I give up + with Leon, I am not 'cause I know I can get him—if I can get Elizabeth out of the picture. *[Whoa, was I going to off her or what?!]* I want Leon soooooooooo bad!

December 28, 1995
Me and Katya went on the internet, and I met this guy, but he thinks I'm fifteen. We are going to be pen pals, he wants my picture, he says he likes me. We are gonna write each other. He lives in Alabama and his name is T.J. Cool hey? But Leon is still my main crush. No one can replace him. He's MY main squeeze. *[I'm actually concerned for Leon's safety at this point.]*

January 2, 1996

Eric told Stephen that he saw me riding in the alley with my friends and smoking. Stephen told Jan, and she was like "our Amanda? Ahhh, no. She's totally against smoking." And it's true, I am a free child of everything like drugs, smoking, beer—alcohol—I am free. I am awesome. *[I sound like I'm fucking high, but . . . very free.]*

January 28, 1996

I am tired, ugly, scrawny and want to go to bed.

February 8, 1996

I wasn't too happy with Janessa. Things aren't really solved. I am just being tossed around everywhere, it feels like she's using me or something, but I don't think she'd do that. "BE NORMAL" is my new Year's resolution. I got a new internet guy named Jamie. *[What is an internet guy? Did I order him off a menu?]*

February 12, 1996

Well what else is new, I am mad at Janessa. She complains that she doesn't want to talk to me 'cause we have nothing to talk about. I am sorry if I don't have a life like her and Katya and Andrea. She has Stephen to blab about all the time (which she does) and Katya has Matt to blab about (which she does) and Andrea has all these guys after her. I am so ugly. Katya + Jan + Andrea are sooooo pretty. I have no life, I am so ugly, dumb, boyfriendless. Why do my friends even hang out with me? Janessa acts like she doesn't care about my life. Only hers and Stephen's. GOD I have no life that I write about my friends' lives. *[Accurate assessment here, Amanda.]*

I ate Kelsey's gum out of her mouth.

February 13, 1996

Tomorrow is the Valentine's dance. Me and Jan had a real fight. Everyone thinks now that I am using Janessa to become popular, but I am not.

February 15, 1996

Andrea said yes to going out with Marko but is going to dump him for Petro. That's really mean. Andrea will probably just dump Petro after an hour or so. Anyway, Janessa and Stephen frenched 3 times today! Holy Man! *[I'm so obsessed with these two kissing. I was clearly jealous.]*

February 21, 1996

Andrea has done some more talking behind my back. I swear it's over between Andrea and I. Tomorrow for sure.

February 23, 1996

MARC IS THE HOTTEST GUY IN THE WORLD BUT I STILL LIKE HIM AND HE'S STILL HOT! And he guarded me *[I'm talking about basketball here]* and I was so close to him that I could touch him. HE IS HOT. *[I have massive concerns about my syntax throughout this whole entry.]*

February 26, 1996

I ate Kelsey's gum out of her mouth.

February 27, 1996

Today me and Kelsey got along really well. *[Well, you did eat the gum out of her mouth.]* It is strange, she seems to actually want to be my friend. I thought she'd be too cool for that or something. *[I clearly think I'm the biggest nerd on the planet and, no surprise, I can't seem to imagine why a nice, smart, pretty girl would ever have any interest in hanging out with me.]*

March 2, 1996

Marc's team was playing basketball after us but I didn't see him. He is such a little hottie. I will sleep and dream of Marc. I love Marc.

March 5, 1996

Katya says I'm being selfish, and she never gets to do anything with Janessa. What can I say though? What difference does it make? I am just a stupid 13 year old, NOT 14 and mature like Katya! I am just a selfish, scrawny, ugly, dumb person. How can any of my friends actually think I am pretty. I am such an ugly repulsive dog. My face is about as attractive as an ass. None of my friends really like me, they all pretend. Life sucks. I can't stand Katya being pissed at me, it's like having a big red pustulating zit ready to pop at the end of your nose. *[Whoa—dark, Amanda. And graphic.]*

March 12, 1996

It still really hurts that Katya and Janessa spent the short day together and I seem like I am not wanted. It may seem really stupid to them but makes me feel really worthless. Amanda Z is becoming my really good friend. I think she is the nicest out of all my friends. We never fight, we always share, she never makes fun of me, she's funny and great to be around. I hope she feels the same way. Kelsey and I are becoming really good friends too. But I feel like I am not popular enough for her. I really like Marc but does he even know who I am?

HOT BOYZ +
HARMONIES

17

"Little Bum, I am the bestest
and you and the second bestest.
My boobs are the BIGGEST.
Love, KWOH (Kristen with orange hair)"

NOTE IN AMANDA'S GRADE 9 YEARBOOK

"... You rock!! I rock!!
Luv ya 4ever, Katie.
PS. My boobs are bigger."

NOTE IN AMANDA'S GRADE 9 YEARBOOK

AT SOME POINT in Grade 8 or 9, Mr. G, my band teacher, informed my parents that I could sing. It meant nothing to me at the time—until the summer going into Grade 10, when I met some boys at the Fringe festival. Okay, truthfully, several were already known to me because I had attended Grade 7 with them: Jason (my locker cleaner) and Toby, who—if you'll remember from the photo caption a while back—said he thought I dressed like I went to private school. There was also another older boy, Jim, whom I didn't recognize. They had an a cappella group called Kokopelli, and since they were pretty cute and had mad harmonizing skills, my girlfriends and I got pretty enamoured. We ended up hanging out with them a bit after seeing a few of their performances, and eventually one of them—a guy named Tony who had flaming red hair and crazy fair skin that was tempting fate even by being out in the sun—suggested that I audition, given that I had done some singing myself with the Kiwanis Music Festival. Turns out choir boys weren't fazed by my weird antics. I had found my niche.

A couple of weeks later, I was auditioning for Kokopelli. I found out that the group had been together for only a year and was made up of people from ages fourteen to twenty-three, which is a really big spread in terms of experience and seemed to bridge whatever hormonal changes a given voice might undergo. The group had a diverse musical repertoire—sacred and secular, ancient and modern, from many different cultures. The artistic director and conductor was animated, supportive, and very keen to pull out whatever voice I had inside of me. At my audition, he placed sheet music on his piano, played me a C, and told me to sing a song I had never heard of before. I didn't think I knew how to read sheet music—which, as it turns out, was what he was trying to find out if I could do—but, somewhere deep down inside me, buried knowledge from my childhood piano lessons came bubbling up, and I found myself singing the notes along the staff as he nodded, snapping a 4/4 time with his fingers.

"You have a lovely voice," he said.

I beamed.

After a few more scales, vocal exercises, and ear training assessments, the conductor got up, closed the lid of the piano, and told me I was in. "You'll be a second soprano," he said, passing me some paperwork.

I couldn't believe it. Either I was decent or this dude let just any freak into his choir.

On my first day with the group, I learned that the people in this choir could sing—like... *really* sing. By my standards, they were also way weirder than I was—I felt transported back into art school among the assortment of tie-dyed wraps, dumpy harem pants, and yogi-inspired jewellery that adorned the necklines around me.

Around that time, I dated Toby, if only for a total of about twenty-four hours. I had my eye on that older boy, Jim, and ended up securing myself a choir boyfriend—and I did it pretty easily, despite all of my past romantic struggles. Jim had frosted tips, small silver hoops in both earlobes, and a spikey tongue ring, and he was *two years older* than I was. And, IMO, he was *super* hot. It was also great that Jim had no

Turns out choir boys weren't fazed by my weird antics. I had found my niche.

My own phone line, my own tray of brownies.
The sugar addiction continues.

idea about my history of being the most hated girl in school. You might recall from the chronology at the start of this book that it was around this time that I experienced my first kiss—with Benny the boob toucher. Jim felt like a fresh start, and I was ready to use my newly earned French-kissing skills. I spent a lot of time talking about him to Bestie Amanda—in fact, he's all I would talk about to Bestie Amanda, because I was now totally boy crazy and had a tendency to ignore any attempt she'd make to turn my attention to her.

That fall, I was starting again at a new school, and for the first time, it wasn't because I had been running away from a throng of tyrants. Junior high was now officially over, and many of us who had attended St. Kevin's ended up at Austin O'Brien High. Grade 9 was tough, but at least I had been at the top of the food chain, if only on an age level. Now, entering high school, I was back at the bottom of a hierarchical system I had no idea how to manage. Still, I had three things going for me:

1 No one had any idea who I was—even those who might have known me by name the previous year. I had shed my nerdy glasses in favour of contact lenses, coloured my hair blond, and learned how to use a flat iron to keep it stick straight. I was now sporting fitted dresses and tight boot-cut jeans.

2 Jim would pick me up after school several days a week, and while we only dated for a few months, it earned me major street cred to have an older boyfriend with his own car.

3 I had a tan Mom would have been proud of.

Within months, I was doing a lot of performances with Kokopelli, both locally as well as out of town. In November, we went "on the road" for nearly ten days and toured as far as Winnipeg, where we performed at the Sturgeon Creek United Church with other choirs from across Canada. One of the choirs was called Tiger Teens, which I thought was a hell of a lot cooler (if less meaningful) than Kokopelli.

Along the way, we stayed overnight in a Mennonite community with a lovely host family who served milk with dinner. Growing up, I had never been served straight-up milk in a glass, ever. While we had cartons of 2% in our fridge, it was strictly reserved for my Shreddies or to act as a base for powdered chocolate. Who would have thought that a trip through the Prairies would end up feeling like such an exotic adventure.

One evening, while we were driving overnight, every other passenger on the bus was asleep except for Jim and me; we were in the back seat, making out. I thought it was all pretty harmless, given that the extent of my "hook up" skills to that point included a bit of gentle kissing and some light, above-the-waist touching. But the next morning, a rumour erupted that there had been moaning coming from the back of the bus and that Jim and I had been having sex. Swathed in their woollen scarves and long jackets, the choir hippies were pissed. Overnight, I went from being the new skinny blond girl to the choir slut—I seriously couldn't catch a break. I may have been sporting a cheap faux leather jacket from Le Château, tight black pants, and black combat boots, but let's be clear: I was a total prude. Jim and I never went past second base.

Concurrently, I was also earning the hatred of Grade 11 and 12 girls back at school—which was, well, inevitable. I had landed the lead in our school musical that year—we were staging *Annie*, which happened to be my absolute favourite. While I shared the lead role with a Grade 12 girl (we would switch nights performing), it was made very clear to me that the older cast members didn't agree that a newbie should be

Let's be clear: I was a total prude. Jim and I never went past second base.

given a lead part, regardless of how well I might sing. I suspect that my acting was comparatively atrocious, and it's true that my newfound vanity meant I had refused to dye my hair red for the part. But thanks to all that intensive vocal training with 'pelli, I *was* able to nail the musical scores. Talent or not, however, a general dislike for me had settled in across what felt like the whole of Grade 12 girldom. And that dislike definitely didn't get any better after my dating life took the same overstep into older-girl territory that my performing life had.

Jim and I had recently broken up, and I had somehow reignited an old crush I had on Janessa's ex, Stephen. That crush went nowhere, but, to my surprise, Stephen's older brother Nick was interested in me, and he—you guessed it—was in Grade 12. A massive upgrade! (And he was Italian.) But this was also perhaps the start of an older-boy trend in my young life that may have led some to make (hilariously false) assumptions about just how much sex I was having. (The true answer: none. Fully dressed dry humping all the way!)

The Grade 12 girls were not happy that I was dipping into their pool of eligible prom dates, and they communicated their distaste by doing things like stealing my clothes when I left them in the theatre changeroom (later to show up at school wearing them like, "Oh, what? This old thing?"). The thing is, I was massively insecure about it all. Nick was a catch: super cute, sweet, romantic, and also one of the best soccer players on the school team. In terms of high school boyfriend quality, I was in the big leagues. We dated for the better part of the school year, and I spent a lot of time at his parents' house, hanging out in his room in the basement— which I remember as having this very cool, grey-toned faux marble effect on the walls. (Later on, in my early dabbles as an interior designer, I tried to imitate this look in my room in teal and purple, and it was an absolute train wreck.)

When Nick asked me to attend his Grade 12 grad with him and his family, I was stoked. Per tradition, the dance was preceded by a shopping spree with my grandmother. In many ways, Grandma could be incredibly conservative, offering up premonitory reminders about protecting my reputation like I was about to have the scarlet letter emblazoned across my soft-pink Club Monaco mohair cardigan. Other times, like this one, she'd do things like let me pick out some sexy and expensive dress to wear out. For the graduation dance, we bought exactly that kind of dress from a store on Jasper Avenue called Who Cares? (Due to a weird chain of events a few years earlier, I had been part of an infomercial for this very store. I never did live it down—anytime a kid would stay up late enough to catch sight of the ad for this high-end local boutique, I'd arrive at school the next morning to have that same kid spit a joyful "Who Cares?" in my face.) The spicy little number that I went home with was a black dress with a tight bodice with bands of mesh that wrapped around and exposed part of my torso, which was pretty racy for a sixteen-year-old. Before we left, Grandma also bought me matching amethyst earrings, a bracelet and necklace, and a new pair of strappy wedges.

The day of the grad dance, I went to the salon, where my soft curls were piled atop my head and pinned in place in a perfect '98 updo. The esthetician powdered my eyelids with lilac to complement my jewellery, gave me a pink lip, and sent me on my way. All in all, I was feeling very sophisticated. That is, until I clambered into my grandfather's olive green four-door Ford Maverick that screamed bloody murder every time you turned the wheel. While Andrea and I used to love being toted around when we were kids, creakily bouncing about in the springy back seats, when it came time for me to learn how to drive, I refused to be caught dead in that thing.

I was feeling very sophisticated. That is, until I clambered into my grandfather's olive green four-door Ford Maverick.

When we were about half a block down the street from Nick's friend's house, I told my grandfather to stop and drop me off.

"Wha…?!" said my grandpa in surprise, cranking up one side of his face (something he still does when he's immeasurably confused about what's coming out of your mouth). "The house is just right up here… I'll drop you off right out front."

"*No!* Please no. Let me out here. I don't want to be seen in this car! It's so embarrassing." I could deal with being dropped off at school in the green monster, but not while I was dressed in that get-up. My grandfather kindly obliged my request and pulled over, and with a "thanks" and an "I love you," I quickly slunk away from the hunk of junk that had just dumped me on the side of the road.

I was safe. As I walked up the street, Nick, his friends, and their Grade 12 girlfriends came into view, along with the limo we all were riding to the dance in. They were all taking photos together in front of it, and just as they were noticing me waving and crossing the street towards them, a loud noise erupted from behind me.

A reh, a reh, a reh, errrrrr.

The green monster, in all of its glory, was pulling a U-ey behind me, the power steering gulping for air and roaring at me to get the fuck out of the way before it plowed me down in its wake.

Reeeeeeeeeeee.

I'm. Going. To. Murder. My. Grandfather.

The Grade 12 girls snickered as I scurried away from the Maverick, pretending like I didn't know the sweet man with the sweet smile who was waving aggressively at me through the window.

I strolled up, my limbs shaking and my cheeks red. "Hey, guys!"

"You look... incredible," Nick said. He pulled me in for a kiss as I nervously looked around to see if the girls were watching. They were. They proceeded to exclude me from their photos as they posed together with their champagne, leaving me standing awkwardly in the background. Knowing that I was insecure about the older girls, Nick pulled me aside to capture a few photos with just the two of us. The consummate gentleman, he grasped my hand and whispered, "*Ti amo*" in my ear, making me feel like the *bella* of the ball.

Crammed in the limo, I looked at Nick and he looked only at me, maybe hoping to get laid that night because that's what people do at prom, right? With my long black cocktail attire, my look was in stark contrast to that of the other girls, who were dressed in the traditional layers of organza, satin, and silk taffeta in Easter egg colours. I like to think that I looked much older, sexy, and sophisticated in a way that screamed, "I landed the hottest guy in Grade 12 and we are going to dry hump later with our prom clothes on!" (Though, much to Nick's dismay, when it came right down to it, I didn't let things get nearly that far that night.)

That summer, shortly after Nick received his acceptance letter to university, he broke up with me.

"We are just going to be in different places," he said.

I knew he was right, and while that helped ease my devastation to some degree, all I could think was that I should have let him touch my boob after grad. After all, he had earned it.

NUMBER 31:
THE ACHING

"P.S. It doesn't bother me when you make fun of me 'cause you're a dipstick anyways."

MARC, Grade 11 love note to Amanda

A note to my readers: I highly recommended listening to "#1 Crush" by Garbage while reading this chapter. It will really set the mood.

WHEN I RETURNED to school in the fall, I learned that two new transfer students were about to join our Grade 11 student cohort. At first, this news didn't faze me, as I was preoccupied with my relief that the belt of my low-rise, boot-cut Buffalo jeans had another year's notch in them, and that maybe the rank of Grade 11 would give me some protection from the mean girls. At sixteen, every penny I earned from my job at Club Monaco went either towards the stash of clothes I had on hold at the back of the store or for some ridiculous Diesel jeans that I couldn't really afford. I blame my grandmother for my love of high-quality threads, as well as for my need to buy multiples of any item that I *really* love.

As I was dodging potential run-ins with the mean girls, my friends were tittering on about these two new students—both boys—who had just started classes with us. We didn't know their names yet but had heard they were both cute, both French (*Canadian*), and both had transferred from another local school in order to join AOB's football team, the Crusaders. As the teachers collected attendance at the beginning of each class, we pooled our information to learn the names of our mystery boys: Marc and Corey. Corey and I shared several classes and it wasn't long before we became fast friends, but it was a few weeks before I had a chance to meet Marc in person.

Sitting on the bleachers after a school assembly one day, a couple of my girlfriends and I started gossiping about the boys.

"Marc is so hot. I'm totally going after him—he's totally mine," announced Katie. She had pretty much dismissed me in Grade 10, but this year she was warming up to me. She had had a good reason for keeping her distance: I had dated her bestie's ex-boyfriend, Mike. He was a professional swimmer and I had acted a bit like scoring him was some sort of feat, but, truthfully, by the end of the year, we had pretty much all dated him.

"Wait... I don't think I've met Marc yet. What does he look like?" I asked.

"He's blond, has blue eyes—sort of looks like a surfer. He plays basketball and football," said Bestie Amanda.

"Wait... Marc what? What's his last name?" My lunch, which typically consisted of poutine, turned in my stomach. *Could it be?*

Katie rolled her eyes in a way only she knew how to do. She was the keeper of all information and had clearly done extra homework to gather all the details we'd need to properly vet these boys (and take them down).

"Marc. Marc with a 'c.' Number 16 on the football team."

"And Number 31 on the basketball team," Danielle chimed in.

At this point, I think my face lost all colour and my mouth probably dropped to the point that my friends thought I had finally decided to experiment with drugs.

"*Marc?*"

"Yeah, and he's French... which means he'll be a very good kisser," said Danielle. She was our token French friend, so we believed her. While the rest of us were struggling through our

"Wait . . . Marc what? What's his last name?" My lunch, which typically consisted of poutine, turned in my stomach. *Could it be?*

language studies, Danielle was very likely whispering sweet nothings into the ears of boys who wanted nothing more than a bilingual bang to add to their high school credit count.

"Marc. *The* Marc?" I was beside myself.

Katie, growing weary of my confusion, launched into detail about how she was going to land Marc as her Grade 11 boyfriend and how none of us could go after him and ruin her chances.

"Katie. I've had a crush on this boy since Grade 8. His basketball team used to practise after my basketball team every Wednesday. I'm like, *totally in love* with this guy. I *have* to go after him."

It was not lost on me that we were treating Marc like a hunting trophy. Katie was furious. Danielle and Bestie Amanda sat silently, giving each other the side-eye as Katie's face started to burn up.

"Oh my *God*, Amanda. Get your own guy! You just go after other people's boyfriends. I like him, and if you go after him he's going to pick you and that's not fair. I saw him first."

"Okay, but seriously, he probably won't even like me, he's *way* out of my league," I said. "Plus, he's going to like who he's going to like. We can't *force* him to like either of us."

Katie wasn't having it. She got up from the bleachers and stormed out of the gym, leaving me dumbfounded. Spirits low, I kept circling in on my worst sense of myself: pimply face, scrawny limbs, and questionable popularity. I determined that my chances of landing Marc would be very slim. But I was going to go for it anyway.

Within two weeks, Marc and I were dating. Katie got over it.

PERHAPS THERE'S some truth in what "they" say about the French ability to seduce and charm—and their casual attitude towards sex. Marc's parents were incredibly cool by my standards, and I often stayed at his place well into the wee hours—even, on occasion, overnight. (I did tell his parents that my family had okayed these sleepovers, but, of course, they knew nothing about them.) At any rate, they didn't seem to have any problem with their little boy taking the opportunity to grow into a man with a girl who clearly didn't have much self-esteem. (I mean, what self-respecting sixteen-year-old girl is staying over at her boyfriend's house? Oh, that's right, *every* sixteen-year-old girl.)

I can't wait to get out of this class to see you. I think you look totally sexy today. And I love your smile so you should stop trying to hide it.

—Marc

Like many teenage boys, Marc smoked a lot of pot. I was *so* against drugs, and when I found rolling papers in his pockets, he'd say, "Those are for my friends"—much like my other friends, who would dodge or hide their casual drug use from me too. In hindsight, I can see how I was only creating a safe place for lies to live. I have legit reasons for hating drugs, but I shouldn't have made it hard for my friends to have fun without my condemnatory eye hovering over them.

Most afternoons, Marc had either basketball or football practice, and I had basketball, soccer, or theatre, so we would usually meet at his house for dinner, generally followed by some heavy petting under his Vince Carter wall poster.

So, what do you want for your birthday? And don't say sex. Frankly, I feel like you're pressuring me just a bit too much. I'm not ready and I think if you truly loved me then you would wait for me.

—Marc

(A note to my grandma: Please stop reading here. I know you worry a lot about my "digital footprint," among other things, and here's where I delve a bit into, well, *sex*.)

MY FIRST *actual* sexual encounter with Marc took place in his upstairs TV room. We didn't just dive right in—in fact, we dragged the process out over days—but once we'd crossed that line, well, game over. I don't remember the actual sex at all, but I think Marc and I can agree that it probably wasn't very good. We were sixteen. What business did we have having sex?

And for the hundredth time my parents aren't going to hate you. Well at least they won't hate you until they find out that you're used goods.

—Marc

At one point I found another girl's panties wedged into the side of his bed—a situation he talked himself out of by blaming it on one of his sisters, claiming they must have been tossed in with his laundry. By that point, I loved him so much that I let it slide.

As you know, when I'm not doing anything, I start thinking about you and then I start to miss you so then I'm forced to go to the bathroom and whack it.

—Marc

During this same time, I ended up befriending a girl in Grade 10 named Jessica—she and Marc had dated in a previous lifetime, but, as I understood it, it had been very casual and they had never slept together. Jessica and I became fast friends during our high school production of *Cats*. (Bestie Amanda never let me live it down that I briefly replaced her with a fancy new friend—but don't worry, the universe paid me back in spades.) The role of Victoria isn't traditionally considered the lead in *Cats*, but she was the striking, elegant kitten who comes of age in the story—and, after the high of getting the lead role in *Annie*, I wanted to be that pussy so badly. Jessica, however, was a gifted dancer, and she ended up winning the role.

The cast and crew of *Cats*.

With her curvy frame, gigantic boobs, long blond hair, big, blue doe eyes, and delicate freckles splashed across her nose, Jessica was a teenage boy's wet dream. Imagine Heather Graham, Jennifer Love Hewitt, and Denise Richards all wrapped up into one tasty, bite-sized snack. That was Jessica. But there was more to her than her nibble quotient, and I was enamoured with her in a way that balanced both admiration and jealousy. It may also have been that because she had once managed to capture the heart of my beloved Marc, I felt the need to keep her close. She was an enemy I had learned to love, and I let my fucking guard down.

I got the role of Grizabella the Glamour Cat, because I had the ability to sing her most famous song, "Memory." While she is traditionally considered a main character, Grizabella is shabby, old, and disgraced, living in the gutter. Foreshadow much?

I think you should stop complaining about Jessica's friends hating you, because every guy in school hates me now cause I'm going out with you.

—Marc

Jessica moved effortlessly across the stage in her tight white unitard, meowing and clawing at the audience. Meanwhile, I was tumbling around in the background like a clumsy cat whose nine lives have all expired. I was a terrible dancer: at one point during rehearsals, it took about half a dozen dancers to show me simply how to sway my hips side to side in a seductive, come-get-me Rum Tum Tugger kind of way. It's a miracle I was ever able to have sex in the first place.

Marc was also in the play. He knew how to tumble a bit from previous gymnastics classes, and it was of course hilarious to watch a football player in tights and ears flip across the stage. Gosh, he *really* must have loved me to have let me convince him to join the play. Or loved my vagina, anyway.

I wrote all of this corny mush-ball crap. But now that I think about it, I don't want to write that crap because you'll think I'm some corny goofball and then you'll dump me. And then when you dump me, I'll realize that I have lost the only thing important to me and that I am a loser, so I'll jump off the Telus tower in hopes you feel guilty for dumping me. So, when you dump me you'll have the guilt of my death on your hands.

—Marc

At some point, rumours started flying about Marc and Jessica. I had a gut feeling they were true. I had confronted Marc several times, but he always assured me that nothing was going on. Eventually, my friends stepped in, literally staging an intervention. They told me that they *knew* Marc was cheating on me with Jessica, but I refused to believe them. One person even told me that once, when Marc was driving me home, Jessica was in the back seat, covered by a blanket. Bullshit, probably, but where there's smoke, there's a teenage girl's face on fire.

Marc and Jessica continued to deny it all, but my faith was starting to crumble. One Friday night, I was staying over at her house in Mill Woods, which was pretty much a straight shot down 50th Street from my house. (A typical suburban home of the late '90s, it had powder-blue vinyl siding and carpets that were vacuumed so regularly, a pattern had formed along its fibres. I was always in awe of those homes with the plush, spotless carpet, wondering if anyone other than the person wielding the vacuum ever entered those flaw-less spaces.) Jessica had stepped out with her mom to run an errand, leaving me alone in the house. That's when I put the plan Bestie Amanda and I had drafted into action: Operation Take This Bitch Down for Hooking Up With My Boyfriend. I went into her parents' room and picked up the telephone. Crouched down on more plush carpet and wedged between the nightstand and the wall, I made my first move.

Looking back, I can't believe I had the chutzpah, but I dialled Ryan, who was Jessica's closest friend, and called on all my years of stage acting to allow me to put on Jessica's voice. I grasped at the carpet, letting the fibres slide through my knuckles as I waited for Ryan to pick up the phone.

"Hello," Ryan barked into the receiver.

Sweetening my voice, I responded, "Hey, Ryan. It's Jessica."

His tone changed and softened to meet mine.

"Hey Jessica... how are you?"

"I'm calling to get some advice because I don't know what to do."

"What's up?"

"Amanda has been asking me about Marc. I don't know what to do..." I paused to see if he'd fill the empty space with something like: *Stop fooling around with your best friend's boy-friend, Jessica.* Instead, he said, "You don't really sound like yourself... are you okay?"

"Yeah, sorry. I'm just trying to be quiet. My parents are in the other room, and I don't want them to hear me talking about this."

This seemed to momentarily quell his concerns. It all felt too easy.

"Do you think she knows about what happened between you and Marc?"

I put the plan Bestie Amanda and I had drafted into action: Operation Take This Bitch Down for Hooking Up With My Boyfriend.

Bingo. Grasping at the rug again, I fell quiet. He had given me just enough proof to justify my concerns.

"Jessica? You still there?"

"I don't know," I responded, wanting him to give me more to work from. "I mean, maybe she knows what I told you."

He didn't bite. In fact, he started to become increasingly apprehensive.

"Jessica, you really don't sound like yourself. Is this you?"

"Of course, it's me. You can see my number on the caller ID." It took everything I had not to shout, *THE JIG IS UP, ASSHOLE! TELL ME ALL THE DETAILS OR I'LL BURN YOUR HOUSE DOWN!!*

Abruptly I blurted out, "'Kay, I gotta go. Amanda is coming, and I think I'm going to tell her the truth."

"Are you sure you want to?"

"I think she already knows."

"Okay, well, call me later and let me know how it goes."

"'Kay, bye, Ryan. And thanks." I hung up the phone. I had everything I needed, but my strategy wasn't to blow my cover with Jessica. At least not yet.

I heard car doors slam outside and I popped up and out of the room, careful to use my socked foot to smooth out the indentations I had made on the carpet. I went to the door and met Jessica and her mom as they came in. Their shared doe eyes welcomed me with a look that said, *You hungry?*

P.S. Don't plan anything for 2 weeks Friday. We can change our "attic fun" to "Fantasyland Hotel Fun." (Hee Hee)

—Marc, realizing my love of theme rooms

I avoided them both for a few weeks after that, until one Saturday afternoon, when Marc came over and picked me up.

He seemed sad and distraught, his lean frame hidden under his heavy jacket. It was a gloomy day, and we were probably both bundled up warmer than we needed to be, our superficial layers acting as protection from emotions that felt foreign and chilly. We drove in silence to a narrow park lining the riverside and found a bench to sit on. It was an odd spot to stop at—the traffic was roaring just behind us and it felt like we were somehow on display.

Like many young women, I longed for the romance that was indoctrinated in me at a very early age. I place most of the blame on Baz Luhrmann's modern adaptation of *Romeo + Juliet*—the one where Claire Danes and Leonardo DiCaprio basically ruin realistic love for every teenage girl on the planet when they discover each other through the fish tank while the song "I'm Kissing You" by Des'ree pulls at your heart strings. Oh... the aching. I still was refusing to believe that the love I shared with Marc could ever be in question—but that didn't stop him from skipping the "drinking poison" part of our Romeo and Juliet story and dumping my sorry ass. The most mortifying thing I remember about this day wasn't being dumped; it was the fact that I had a cold, and so I was red-faced and snotty while trying to look super cute. I mean, how was I supposed to win Marc back if I was using the arm of my winter jacket like a three-year-old whose mom couldn't be bothered to wipe her nose? I probably should have demanded more answers from him, but all I could think about was maintaining my composure. (See, no issues with vulnerability here, folks!)

I will say that, many years later, when we were both single again, Marc's path and mine intersected again when I drove to Edmonton for a friend's stagette and decided to ring him up (read: booty-call him). We met with a few friends at the Iron Horse bar, and I spent the night flirting shamelessly

with a different old friend until Marc showed up. We proceeded to have fun, drunken sex, and it was the closest thing
I've ever had to a one-night stand. But that was much, much
later. As my first truly heartbreaking split was happening, it
didn't feel like there would be a "later." Like all breakups, no
matter how many times we experience them, it felt like the
absolute end of the world.

P.S. NO FRENCH CANADIANS were harmed in the making
of this chapter.

19

Y2 NOT ~~OK~~

:(

"It really hurts me to hear you say some of the things you say. Don't take this the wrong way but I'm really tired of hearing how ugly you are and how nobody likes you and how you always look like shit. I'm really tired of it... I can't keep telling you over and over how beautiful you are."

BESTIE AMANDA, Grade 12 intervention letter

RETURNING FOR my senior year of high school, I really felt like it was finally going to be my moment. I had taken to buying clothes from GapKids because I could get more bang for my (grandmother's) buck. My shopping plan that fall was to show Marc what he had been missing all summer. Despite the lingering frost and the goosebumps that kept company with the fading summer freckles that still danced on my nose, I was not deterred from showing up at school in a cropped white T-shirt, short black skirt, light puffy vest, and platform sandals—all designed to show off the sculpted legs I had earned through summer league soccer and a killer tan built up through a combination of sun beds, tanning oil sessions with Mom, and many hours at the Mill Creek outdoor pool with Bestie Amanda. After cutting through the fabled Capilano Mall and grabbing a samosa with some change I had pilfered from my grandfather's coin stash, I was usually a little hypothermic by the time I reached school. Trouble was, Marc was already dating a scrappy Grade 10 girl who had an older brother in our graduating class. She was from the "wrong side" of the North Saskatchewan River, and she had no qualms about attempting to make my senior year a complete nightmare. Channelling a Spice Girls vibe in a pre–Ariana Grande world, she wore her hair the same way every single day: slicked back into a crisp ponytail, except for long bangs parted in the middle that were expertly swept under the chin of her round face. She may have barely hit the "must be this tall to ride" mark, but she and her friends seemed to tower in size as they snickered and pointed at me in the main hall every day.

The year started as most years did: with me committing to way too many extracurricular activities in the pursuit of gaining approval as a massive overachiever. Right off, I started my campaign for student council president. Given that the school didn't have a cheer team, student government was clearly the next popularity power move... right? The thing is, I had zero expectation that I was going to win. My friend Corey, who is much more likeable and played on the football team (Go Crusaders!), was running against me, so, in a classic underdog move, I based my entire campaign strategy on how I was going to besmirch my opponent. "He just simply won't have time to take this seriously, you know, with all of that practice and those away games," I would say. This was a bullshit tactic, of course; I was known to play on about seven sports teams each school year, and I participated in another half-dozen school clubs, ranging from debate team and the newspaper group to drama club and grad council.

Much to my surprise, however, the angle worked. The student body voted me in. But despite reaching my goal, I immediately translated that sign of popularity into a sign of pity, knowing that it was because I was the only person in the school who gave two shits about Crusader spirit. Still, I proceeded to flex a high-level agenda, which included a tropical-themed Rookie Week, Halloween Hypnotist Wayne Lee, a glam Christmas dance with an MTV DJ, a toy drive for at-risk kids (which ended up reaping three hundred stuffed animals), and a Stress Reliever Week to help combat concerns about any impending Y2K fallout. (If you are young enough

In a classic underdog move, I based my entire campaign strategy on how I was going to besmirch my opponent.

to have missed the whole Y2K era, it was basically mass hysteria around the belief that computers would implode when their two-digit digital calendar programs turned over from 1999 to 2000.) In addition to all this, I was awarded the lead for that year's school play—*Peter Pan*—and my co-lead, Kyle, dropped out early in the process, citing "creative differences." And through it all, I had to deal with frequent run-ins with Jessica because she not only ended up acting as secretary for student council but also landed the role of Wendy to my Peter Pan. Our drama teacher, Mrs. S-H, had a sick sense of humour.

Early in the year, I was among a group of students selected for the opportunity to attend an off-campus retreat at a site called Camp Oselia, with the intent that we would dig deep into some spiritual shit and get a better sense of what we wanted for our futures. The weekend started off poorly, when I arrived at our shared bunks and saw that all of my friends had moved to another room, leaving me alone. In my sour mood, still-painful flashbacks of lunches alone in a pre-friend era rose up, and my insecurities flared up like a cystic acne breakout. It probably felt like all my friends were finally turning on me—because I knew they always would—and so, I turned into the worst version of myself: abrasive, negative, and dismissive.

It became my mission to use my nasty, contagious energy to spoil everything and everyone around me. I started off by picking an unnecessary fight with my core group of friends, quickly replacing them with a few outliers who were more impressionable and easily influenced. Even the teachers at the camp, all of whom had generously volunteered their time, could see how my acidic mood was rippling throughout the group of girls, causing massive disruption and burning everything in its wake—and it royally pissed them off. (I didn't realize how badly until I returned to school after this tumultuous weekend and found myself scorned by many of the teachers who had previously been my biggest fans.)

But it wasn't all for nothing. The effect my rotten attitude was having on the whole camp made me realize that I had more power than I'd thought, and that maybe, just maybe, it was time for me to reconsider my worth (and give Bestie Amanda a break from hearing me bitch about it while I was at it). So, I dug in further, pushed further, did more. Did too much—of everything except what I was supposed to be doing.

One day about this time, one of those same teachers whom I had disappointed—Mr. W—stopped me in the hall.

"Where are you rushing off to?" he asked. I'm sure I responded with some comment that stank of "I don't have time for this." Something like: "I'm heading to [insert somewhere in school that wasn't class] to take care of [insert something that shouldn't have been taking precedence over my studies]."

His fluffy brows furrowed. "You're going to burn out... have a breakdown."

I had no idea what he was talking about. What did a breakdown look like? Was he speaking from experience? In a time that was less "woke," it was assumed that mental breakdowns were just for crazy old people ("old" being anyone over thirty-five).

"Gotta go!" I said. I scurried away, late for whatever had me skipping English class. In my mind, Mr. W was simply projecting his own stress onto me.

Because I was *solid*.

Then, I almost flunked out of high school.

Mr. W had not been wrong. I had stretched myself so thin that I went from getting a decent share of As with enough credits to graduate an extra student to putting myself at risk for not graduating at all. When first-term report cards were released, a glaring 49 percent in English shone out from the

Fucking up in English was not an option in the Whelan Clan.

page. English had once been my best class, but I had taken to skipping it, along with its prescribed homework. (A very big risk, because when any of us showed up with incomplete homework, our English teacher, Mrs. D, would separate us from the class and lecture to only those who had done the work, calling the rest of us "turkeys.") The thing was, that homework consisted mostly of dated fiction that predominantly bored me. Shakespeare continued to plague my life, but this time I was the one considering drinking poison as our teacher made us memorize and recite Hamlet's "To be, or not to be" soliloquy. Sure, it allowed me to parade my theatrical flair, but I knew it certainly wouldn't come in handy when I sat down to write my first job application.

Fucking up in English was not an option in the Whelan Clan. My aunt, who took pleasure in correcting my words on the daily, and my grandmother, who took pleasure in her own use of metaphors, immediately booked an appointment with Mrs. D. With their significant knowledge of (and clout in) the school system, they started quoting curriculum requirements to my teacher and demanded to know why she had never reached out with her concerns.

Smug, Mrs. D explained, "From my perspective, students need to learn independence and take responsibility for their actions and choices."

My aunt's response: "While we do agree that Amanda needed to complete her homework, her actions and choices have also included being student body president, volunteering as a D.A.R.E. representative, and taking the lead in the school play, among many other commitments. She contributes significantly to this school and the community."

Tapping at the table with a pencil, Mrs. D crossed her legs, then uncrossed them, then resorted to a firmer stance, with both feet firmly on the floor.

"Karen, while those are activities all well and good, they are not required parts of the school curriculum. That is not independence."

Aunt Karen saw an opening and dove in. "While I would maintain that Amanda showcases incredible independence, arguably, interdependence is a far greater skill," she said. My grandmother, nodding in agreement, didn't just back up this defence but actually took it to the "philosopher's debate" level by adding, "We aren't alone in this world; we rely on others."

But Mrs. D was resolute. "The fact is that Amanda has not attended all her classes. She came unprepared for the classes she did attend. She did not complete her homework. She prioritized her extracurricular activities over her studies. And now she is paying the price," she said. "Amanda is almost an adult. Failing this class falls on her and her alone."

Crushed by my sense of inadequacy, I broke down and started crying. My aunt, tossing her head of thick, wild red curls, told me to leave the classroom. Through the doors, I could hear her absolutely lose it on Mrs. D... philosophical debate over and done. Twenty minutes later, when my aunt and grandma joined me in the hall, they were both visibly upset.

"You've been given the opportunity to submit a make-up essay and complete a make-up exam to improve your grade. Let's go," Aunt Karen said as we walked out of the school.

Going into the Christmas holidays, when I should have been reading whatever book was so boring that it was leading me to neglect my grades, a relentless case of recurrent tonsillitis that had been plaguing me for months finally brought me down. Delirious from dehydration, I landed in the emergency room, where I passed out in a wheelchair. When I woke up, I was being pumped full of fluids through an IV jammed into the back of my hand. For the next few weeks, I had to return to the hospital every eight hours to have my veins refreshed with an elixir of antibiotics—"the drip," as the nurses called it—and Mr. W's "I told you so."

After I recovered, my aunt Karen offered a rather heavy hand on the make-up paper I had written for Mrs. D, along with a bit of study assistance for my second shot at the test. Given that she had just obtained her PhD in elementary education, I was sure I was going to ace the essay and crush the re-test. Alas, Mrs. D, still furious about having her teaching abilities questioned, took this opportunity for a little retaliation. My PhD-level essay earned a grade in the low 60s, and as Mrs. D was bent on making her point, the exam included questions like "What was the middle name of the street vendor that the main character looked at while passing by but who had absolutely no impact on the storyline?" and "Was the main character's mother's sister's husband's daughter's doll a brunette or blonde?" But despite Mrs. D's little "lesson," my grade ended up being decent enough that I was no longer at risk of being shunned by my family for not being able to attend university.

Meanwhile, I had replaced quarterback Marc with boob-toucher Benny, the class clown. We were an unlikely match, but I was drawn to his sense of humour and seemingly "bad boy" ways. It was while I was seeing him that I first tried alcohol—on the weekend before my eighteenth birthday. It was a little bizarre to have stayed away from booze for so long only to break the rules with just a few days left until legal age, but why be predictable. Hanging out with Benny at his dad's creepy house in Beaumont, I let him egg me on to drink two Mike's Hard Lemonade coolers while we blasted rap music, and by the time he drove me home, I was tipsy (yes, this is the scene you might recall from the chronology at the start of the book when I was screaming out Eiffel 65's "Blue (Da Ba Dee)" in Benny's dad's F150).

On my actual birthday—the Thursday of the following week—Bestie Amanda and I put on outfits that she called "hoochie in a non-hoochie sort of way" and spent the better part of the evening in a lineup to get into Cowboys Bar for their "25 Cent Draft Beer" special (though what we really wanted were Vodka Slimes). We never made it in and instead ended up hanging out with some older boys in their crazy souped-up lowriders. As we sat in the back seat, the boys bounced the cars on their hydraulics down the main drag of Whyte Avenue. We ended up at some dive bar where I proceeded to smash back a couple of Singapore Slings before becoming anxious about getting up for school the next day. I was taking school seriously again, but despite feeling like I was finally out of the woods, the year culminated in a serious slap in the face. I had missed my opportunity to secure the biggest honour of all: valedictorian.

Yes, while all my extracurriculars had earned me the opportunity to sashay across the gymnasium stage at year-end in a fitted white sundress patterned in little blue flowers to accept the Crusader Service medal and the Drama Queen award, those wins paled in comparison to the big prize. But I had dug too deep a hole with my post-camp behaviour, and the role of valedictorian was awarded to a very bright girl named Carol. I remember that after the announcement, one of the teachers pulled me aside to explain that, even after all of the contributions I had made during high school, my grades "simply weren't good enough"—not even to make the nominee list. It was then that I realized I had sacrificed my biggest dream in pursuit of another goal altogether: people-pleasing.

So, I simply doubled down on my friendship with Bestie Amanda. Together, we embraced our transition into adulthood by becoming obsessed with our graduation dresses and

On my birthday, Bestie Amanda and I put on outfits that she called "hoochie in a non-hoochie sort of way."

#FitCheck.

what life in university was going to look like. I even offered to share Benny with her at graduation when she didn't have a date. Dressed in an electric-blue gown that cascaded into a mermaid flare at my calves, I again looked exceptionally out of place that night. Much like when I went to Nick's prom, the other girls there had mostly taken a different approach, this time donning princess-cut gowns in soft pastel colours. As was typical, stepping in to sort me out and hold up the family standards, my grandmother ensured I had matching electric-blue snakeskin strappy sandals and blue-coloured jewellery to match my dress, and with her help, I pulled together a statement look that I can still think back on with pride today.

The rest of the evening, not so much: the night started with me having to listen to Carol give "my" valedictorian speech, and ended with me sitting on the sideline of a terrible bonfire party, feeling alone, alienated, and unloved, unable to find Bestie Amanda and getting occasional reports that Benny was off somewhere kissing other girls (which may or may not be true). From there, things went seriously south, and my senior year inevitably ended as it should have: with a can of beer being poured over my head by the boob toucher.

AM I ENDING THIS BOOK in too sad a place? My editors and peer reviewers certainly thought so. "Give us some hope," said one. "You're a very successful entrepreneur who is loved by many." Another said, "This cuts a bit too deep... lighten it up a bit and bring it back to the reason why you're a shithead. ☺" That's the thing, though: despite the fact that I have the support of amazing friends, a job I love and do well, and a family who would go to the ends of the earth for me, I have never, to this day, been able to shake that lingering notion that I am, well, *not that likeable.* I think anyone who spent time as an outlier in their younger years can relate. No matter what success comes our way later in life, many of us share a common attachment to our formative years.

At this point, you've learned about my period, my boobs, and my bathroom habits, so it seems a bit unlikely that I'll be able to convince you that I don't still find myself seeking the approval of others. Why do we care so much? The need to feel loved, to *be* loved, is universal, and we all see the world through a series of our own stories, each providing an opportunity to reflect, reframe, and rewrite ourselves. This act in and of itself is an inherently empowering process. It's how we own ourselves—how we define ourselves in the world.

The failure to find my self-worth in the opinions of others created a sort of emotional dysmorphia that followed me into adulthood. I had made myself so busy that I couldn't see the vibrant young woman I had transitioned into—even when my friends (notably Bestie Amanda) tried to show her to me. In my own eyes, I was still an awkward, pimply-faced teenager searching for her place. Even today, that drive still controls me—for better and for worse. I'm often asked, "Amanda, *how* do you do it all?" My incessant energy (fuelled by my need to live up to my ridiculously high and fully self-imposed standards of success) is often interrogated in a manner, perhaps not always complimentary, that makes me wonder if I should try practising a life that's a little *less* inspired. As a teenager, I had innocently assumed that, once I graduated, the mean girls would simply go away. I could move to another city; I could redefine myself at will. If I excelled professionally—if I *made it*—I would earn respect. But I was seeking validation in all of the wrong places. So I don't look in those places anymore. Or, at least, I try not to.

The truth is, some people will love you for the same reasons others will hate you. And in the worst of times, you will

Grad photo. Would you check those chunky highlights?

cross paths with those whose only purpose is to dull your shine. If we listen to these "haters," we'll only learn to mute ourselves, to remain quiet so as not to bring attention to what makes us the best version of who we are. At times, I have been guilty of muffling or censoring my own voice in an attempt to please. Writing this book seems to be an act of correcting this, to some extent.

So, speaking of pleasing (my editors, in this case), how do I give you that hope? I'd like to think this entire narrative is *all* about hope—that you have seen a little bit of yourself in these stories and have laughed along the way at how stupid life can be sometimes. Maybe my particular story is weirder than it is tragic, but there are lessons I've learned along the way that I would never trade in for a life of normal (whatever *that* means...). And even if it's making me literally cringe to actually write this, if you will indulge me for just a moment, can I say that these experiences have shaped me into a resilient, tenacious, independent, and confident woman? One who, even still, on occasion will doubt herself, of course. But while life might have felt insurmountable to fifteen-year-old me, I've come out the other side grateful for all I have experienced.

I'm still a little odd. Maybe not liked by all. But in my own little way, I am sharing my story—or, at least, the stories that I have told myself—so that you too might find the courage to leave whatever (weird little) mark you want to leave on the world.

FYI, MR. W: I still haven't had a breakdown. Not yet.

ACKNOWLEDGEMENTS

FEEL PRETTY LUCKY that despite being a walking anti-bullying advertisement, I made it out of those years alive. In some way, the people below have all contributed to bringing this crazy idea of writing a book to life.

To my obnoxiously loud multi-generational family, who raised me like a pack of wolves and inspired my lifelong love affair with reading and writing: Thank you for always unapologetically correcting my grammar—it has finally come in handy. I trust that I have spilled enough sailing and *Star Trek* metaphors throughout this book to make you proud. Consider the stories within these pages as payback for all the times you called me "Stinky Feet" since that year I forgot to bring socks on our sailing trip in the San Juan Islands. For fuck's sake, I was seven; someone, *anyone*, should have packed them for me. Gramps, Grams, Mama, Uncle Bobby, Aunt Karen, and Uncle David: I owe you big-time. Thanks for making sure I didn't drown in a gutter.

An additional thank you to my mother, Deborah Whelan: This story would not have been possible without your beautifully wild life. I know you sometimes felt you were never enough, but you have so much to be proud of—me (duh)—and you never stop reminding me of just how proud you really are. While this book shares my experiences through my eyes, I have always felt you have your own story to tell, and it is yours alone. My hope is that one day you'll share your own stories.

To my publishing crew at Page Two: Jesse Finkelstein, thanks for taking a risk on this weird memoir. I fell in love with you on our first call, and my gut knew that your team was the right fit. You knew just when to send me a supportive email throughout the process, and I'm certain I'm your most annoying author.

To my editor Amanda Lewis, who has a deep love for memoirs, cats, and trees: I quickly realized that we are nerd soul sisters and believe that had I found you sooner, my lunch hours might not have been so lonely. I asked you to hold me to a very high standard to ensure my book wasn't a massive dumpster fire, so if people don't like this book, as promised, I will forward all email from hatemail@notthatlikeable.com to your personal inbox.

To my editor Melissa Edwards, who picked up my book during the second half of editing because I went on a sabbatical from writing and Amanda Lewis went on a sabbatical to write a book on big-tree tracking (yes—you heard me right): I was nervous at first to be working with a new editor so late in the process, but you proved your editorial prowess on your very first pass of the book. You managed to maintain my voice while bringing clarity for the reader, and for this, I am thankful beyond words.

To my copyeditor, Steph VanderMeulen: I didn't think it was possible to keep striking gold with every woman who helped bring this book to fruition, but there you were, dropping F-bombs, zealously sharing in the '80s and '90s nostalgia, and keeping pace with my weird emails from day one. Thanks for letting me "die on that hill" over the use of "bold-face" over "bald-face." It really was keeping me up at night. [Copyeditor's note: Fuck yeah. I gotchu, AmHam. Also, long live Fun Dip, frosty pink eyeshadow, and Herbal Essences!]

Much thanks as well to the rest of my Page Two team: Chris Brandt (for fielding our crazy marketing questions and being patient when I fell on and off the map during the process), Adrineh Der-Boghossian (for managing me like a child as I missed every single deadline), Taysia Louie (for nailing the design layout on your first go), and proofreader Alison Strobel (who I'm sure loved how many times I asked, "Do we need a comma here?").

To the Gentle Lion team who have supported "The World of AH" and all my crazy ideas: When I informed you that I was writing a book, you never flinched and instead were eager to support me right to the end. You are truly an extension of my brand, and much of my success is thanks to your unwavering commitment to being our biggest cheerleaders.

To my peer review team: Rachelle Babcock (thanks for making sure that "Cock Tease" didn't make it through the edits), Erin Whelan (you married into a weird family), Lana Rogers (for finding my blind spots), Jeff Jamieson (for reassuring me I could easily weave in a story about pooping myself), and Amanda Nordstrom (my longest-standing friend, pleasantly harshest critic, fact checker, and biggest fan. I wish you had shown up more in this book, but honestly, I couldn't even begin to tackle the depth of our friendship together— we were too busy having fun).

To the AHID team and community: It has crossed my mind that this book is TMI, but I'm going to practise what I preach: if this is too much for you, we probably wouldn't like each other IRL much anyway. One of the things I feel the proudest of is the community of people who support our studio and the team I have the honour of leading. It is my greatest treasure. (Special shout-out to rockstars Courtney Molyneaux and Sara Swallow who supported with creative assets for NTL's social platforms, pre-order campaign, and website, among other last-minute requests!)

To my friends: I won't list all of your names because if I miss one of you, I'm never going to hear the fucking end of it. Thanks for putting up with me talking about writing this book for so damn long, and then, I hope, finally buying it when it came out much later than it should have. I was probably busy drinking Spritz with you instead of editing my manuscript, so really, it's your fault.

To all of the people who appeared in this book and to those brave souls who allowed me to use their real names to preserve the integrity of the stories: thank you. I can't wait to hear your version of the story. (For those of you who didn't, I get it—no one wants to be nicknamed "the boob toucher.")

To the team at Cardinale (and to the teams at the rest of the bars around the globe where I have sat creating this exposé): Thank you for pouring me endless tasters so that I could craft my first draft partially intoxicated. As Ernest Hemingway so eloquently said, "There is nothing to writing. All you do is sit down at a typewriter and bleed." He also said, "Write drunk, edit sober," which I have done (for the most part). Thanks for letting me bleed all over your restaurant and hiding me in the middle room, away from distracting creeps (not you, the other guys).

To the funny women authors who came before me and inspired me with their weird and fucked-up stories so I would share my own, among them a few of my faves: Kelly Oxford, Busy Philipps, Samantha Irby, Amy Schumer, and Chelsea Handler.

And finally, to my bullies: Please feel free to leave a positive review of this book on your favourite online retailer's website or online forum. I mean, it's the least you could do. Alternately, e-transfers are being accepted for my extensive therapy at sorry@notthatlikeable.com. ✌

Posing on Grandpa's creaky green Maverick.

ABOUT THE AUTHOR

AMANDA HAMILTON is a Canadian author, creative entrepreneur, and the founder of Amanda Hamilton Interior Design and Palette Archives—and, after the publication of this memoir, she is certain to be on the outs with several of her friends, family members, and clients. You can find her lit by the glow of her laptop at various bars across the globe, likely posting something weird about her love for Crocs, her desire for a raccoon, or her eternal devotion to her long-legged, greasy-bearded companion, Liam the Irish wolfhound, on Instagram: **@AmandaMHamilton**.

WANT TO STAY CONNECTED?!
I SURE DO

NOW THAT YOU KNOW my humble roots, darkest secrets (hi, Solo Booby!), and bathroom habits, let's not pop a squat there! I'd love to continue the conversation, connect, and swap horror stories because well, shit, life is pretty crazy. Let's connect + I'll bring some candy.

Visit My Websites

notthatlikeable.com

amandahamilton.ca

Find Me on Social

 @TheRealAmandaHamilton

 @AmandaMHamilton and @NotThatLikeable

 @AmandaMHamilton

 @TheRealAmandaHamilton

Hire Me

Need a keynote speaker? A Master of Ceremonies? Maybe you're in the market for an engaging (and funny) panelist? A new best friend? I'm your gal!

Reach Out!

You can find me at **press@amandahamilton.ca.**

Jazzed about This Book?

I'd be forever grateful if you left a review (or a love note) via your preferred online retailer's website or online forum.

Alternatively, you can scan this QR code to leave your warm words. Reviews have never been easier.

CPSIA information can be obtained
at www.ICGtesting.com
Printed in the USA
BVHW082331060323
659779BV00001B/6